HIGH IMPACT TEAMING

HIGH
IMPACT
TEAMING

STEFAN DECUYPER
ELISABETH RAES
ANNE BOON

LANNOO
CAMPUS

SLOW DOWN
TO GO FASTER

D/2020/45/301 – ISBN 978 94 014 6997 5 – NUR 807, 808

COVER DESIGN   Gert Degrande | De Witlofcompagnie
INTERIOR DESIGN Banananas.net

LannooCampus Publishers is a subsidiary of Lannoo Publishers, the book and multimedia
division of Lannoo Publishers nv.

LannooCampus Publishers
Vaartkom 41 box 01.02   P.O. Box 23202
3000 Leuven   1100 DS Amsterdam
Belgium   Netherlands
www.lannoocampus.com

CONTENTS

This book is dedicated to Paul Stinckens,

Olympic kayaker and founder of Unicorn.

PROLOGUE: WHY 'I'?

The first words of this book date back to the 2nd of March 2010. I wrote them on the back of an envelope, in a strange house in a strange city about 145 km east of Mexico City.

My quest for the essence of teamwork, however, began much earlier than just one decade ago. First, I studied for fifteen years at the University of Leuven, Belgium: ten years of educational sciences and five years of organizational psychology. Afterwards, I successfully finished three PhDs on team learning.[1] Then, I gained over fifteen years of experience as a team coach, mostly within Unicorn, a company that supports teams at CXO level throughout Europe (www.unicorngroup.com).

Before you start reading my book, there is just one small thing you should know: 'I' don't exist. You might have noticed that this book cover cites three authors: Stefan Decuyper, Elisabeth Raes, and Anne Boon. The *I* addressing you here is the aggregate of these three people.

> *There is no I in team...*
> *But there sure is one in teaming.*
>   *– I*

We wrote this book together and chose to write it in the first person singular because we believe that the stories come across better that way. But there is a second reason. It is very likely that you have heard the saying, '*There is no I in team'*. The *I* in this quote refers to the first person, suggesting *the team* is more important than the individuals in the team. But you never bump into a team in the hallway, do you? You don't run into teams, you run into one, two, or three individuals. People expect far too much of *the team*. But *the team* isn't doing anything. Maybe there is no *I* in team but there sure as hell is one in *Teaming*. High Impact Teaming always starts with an individual, an *I*. An

I takes the initiative to ask others how they see the situation in order to start constructing a shared vision. An *I* shows vulnerability, admits that he or she was wrong and rebuilds psychological safety. An *I* challenges, starts the *good fight,* and the result is that the team achieves better results together.

Sometimes, people ask us, '*You wrote a book on High Impact Teaming. So tell me, were you guys a perfect team?*' Well, that single question reveals just about everything that is wrong with how we are educated on teamwork. We are promised formulas for collaboration that will solve all our problems. Let me tell you a little secret: the way we collaborated was far from problem-free because collaboration never is. The difference between theory and practice is always bigger in practice than it is in theory. It doesn't matter how much expertise you have on the topic or how well you have worked together in previous collaborations. Teams never start off great. Effective teams just keep on figuring out how to improve. Step by step, they create their own formula for success. Not just once, but again and again and again.

Now that we have finished this book and the dust has settled, we can clearly see how that is exactly what we did. How each of us made big mistakes and how we did everything we could to fix them. How our team and each individual in it benefited from the struggles we faced and conquered. How the result is an example of what three individuals can achieve when they write and rewrite their own formula for effective collaboration: a book without compromises. Written from one pen. That is why we use *I*.

INTRODUCTION

Text Message 1: '*Dad is in hospital. There's something wrong with his heart.*'

Text Message 2: '*Everything OK, though. Visitors allowed.*'

Text Message 3: '*He is in Sacred Heart Hospital, room 402.*'

On our family WhatsApp, my mother's messages inform us about my father's hospitalization. The three messages reveal exactly the one thing she is trying to hide: panic. I suddenly feel my heart in my throat and my hands shake while I type: '*I'm on my way.*' About 30 minutes later, I knock on the door. '*Come in,*' Mom says. Her eyes are swollen. My father looks tired and his face is a bit red. '*Everything is under control,*' he softly growls. He does what fathers do: he reassures me. Just when I am about to ask what happened, two nurses enter the room. Their name tags read Stephanie and Kelly.[2] They tell us it is time for a bedside briefing because the new shift has started, and ask my father whether it is okay for him that we stay in the room. He nods. While Stephanie explains the situation to Kelly – what has already happened and what still needs to be done – I feel my body beginning to relax again. My breath moves from my breast to my stomach. The first tests were not 100% conclusive, but at first sight there is no acute danger.

My attention is drawn to what has always fascinated me: people who collaborate. It seems a bit unusual to me that Stephanie and Kelly debrief the shift in the presence of the patient. Stephanie explains. Kelly listens and asks questions. At some point, my father interrupts to make an additional comment: '*Stephanie took my blood pressure and it dropped from 18 over 10, to 14 over 8.*' After a few minutes, the nurses leave the room. '*They never used to do these kinds of debriefings with the patient in the room,*' my father says. '*At least I know now that a new nurse is in charge and I feel reassured that all the information has been transferred to her. Back in the day, we didn't have a clue.*'

It is true. They didn't do that before. In numerous cases, crucial information disappeared in the gap between two shifts. Necessary adjustments in medications didn't always happen. People died as a result. Not as a result of bad intentions, nor as a result of incompetent staff, but as a result of work processes that no one really questioned.[3] Today, the work flow in this hospital is different. After my visit, I asked one of the nurses how their new methods of working had arisen. With a proud look in her eyes, she told me that the change had not occurred after the intervention of expensive consultants. They had developed the new method themselves. A nursing colleague had read about it and presented the basic idea at one of the team meetings.[4] The head nurse reacted enthusiastically. *'We decided to test it for a while and now it is our new normal. Bedside briefings take the same amount of time as before, but you can do certain tasks, like checking the intravenous drip, alongside one another. When you are in the room in the presence of the patient, the information you transfer tends to be more accurate. And sometimes, when we forget something, patients complete the information themselves.'*[5]

That is what this book is about: **H**igh **I**mpact **T**eaming. Or, to put it more simply: team learning with impact. Learning how to collaborate more effectively, more efficiently and more consciously. Of course, High Impact Teaming is not always a matter of life and death. In fact, most of the time it isn't. Most of the time, it is about small things, small improvements. The difference between bad and a bit less bad or good and a bit better. It is about a short conversation here and a little intervention there.

High Impact Teaming isn't rocket science, but the devil is in the detail. This book explains that the biggest differentiator of top teams and other teams is to be found in these details. It's about *how* they slow down just for a moment to go faster afterwards. *How* they stop together to think. *How* they improve the psychological safety in the team, the shared vision, or the team organization. *How* they ensure that good ideas from outside the team find their way in. *How* they talk about what is going on beneath the surface.

We can all remember that one great moment in the life of the team that changed everything. That single team conversation that seemed to reboot the hard drive and got you and your colleagues up and running again. Scientists call those moments turning points. But at the same time, we all know there is no silver bullet for improving teamwork. We all know that hits are never made overnight. That success is always the result of a cumulation of moments.[6] During my doctoral research, I studied turning points, and the truth is that the big moments we tend to remember are always preceded by many small ones that we tend to forget. So turning points are more like tipping points. It is hard to create them consciously and they often arise when we least expect them.

> *Life can only be understood backwards, but it must be lived forwards.*
>
> *– SØREN KIERKEGAARD*[7]

In contrast to those big moments, the small moments *can* be created consciously. Those small improvements are within our circle of influence. I will never forget how the coach of the Dutch women's hockey team drilled his team on the value of small improvements: *'50 times two percent is 100 percent too.'*[8] This book reveals how effective teams improve their own formula for success, percentage by percentage. They do so by continuously creating little moments of slowing down to go faster.[9] That's how they manage to live *forwards*. By tackling small problems and opportunities step by step.

Now, you all work with other people. Sometimes you call them team mates or group members. Sometimes you call them colleagues or stakeholders. It doesn't matter what you call them. One thing is certain. This book is not just about how standard *teams* learn to collaborate more effectively. It is about how you can improve any kind of short- or long-term collaboration. It doesn't matter whether you give that collaboration the name team, group, division, company, or any other name. As long as your collective has some kind of desire to accomplish something together, this book is written for *you*.[10] And you *don't* need to be the formal leader, the manager, or the coach. It's okay if you are. It's okay if you're not. This book is about how anyone in or around the collective can influence its effectiveness.

> *Reading is like sex: sure, it may give some practical results, but that's not why we do it.*
>
> *– ADJUSTED FROM RICHARD FEYNMAN*

In the first chapter, I present the *High Impact Teaming model* in a nutshell. In the subsequent chapters, I deepen each of its components. Along the way, I present a number of models and tips and tricks for improving team effectiveness.[11] However, I am compelled to end the introduction of this book with a disappointing message. You will not learn anything new. Somehow – at some level – you already know all of it. The only thing this book has to offer is a science-based mirror. And the sole purpose of that mirror is to help you reflect on your own mindset about effective collaboration. Reflections on how to frame and clarify what you already know. Reflections on those things you might have lost sight of. *'That sounds pretty ambitious. I seriously doubt that you will be able hold up a mirror to me.'* I hear you. You are right. I cannot confront you with a mirror. But you can. Just read this book with yourself and your team(s) in mind. *'And what if that doesn't work?'* Well, just in case, there is a plan B. Along with my colleagues from Unicorn and the University of Leuven, I created a free online questionnaire based on the High Impact Teaming model (www.teammirror.eu).[12] With just three clicks of your mouse, you can set it up for any team. You only need the email addresses of the team members, a deadline for completing the questionnaire, and a moment to discuss the results together. Two days before that meeting, all team members automatically receive their individual Team Mirror report. The Team Mirror reflects how you and your colleagues see the team and where there are opportunities for High Impact Teaming.

CHAPTER 1:
THE HIT MODEL

Books and articles about teamwork usually start in more or less the same way. First, the author emphasizes that teamwork has become broadly accepted as the best way for organizations to cope with the rapid changes in contemporary society. Then, the author offers convincing proof that he or she has read most of the existing literature and earned a few stripes in the world of working with teams. The introduction ends with a convincing suggestion that the author has discovered the holy grail: a handful of variables which, when assembled correctly, comprise the magic formula for effective teamwork.

Control + alt + delete.

The key message of this book is fundamentally different. I can understand why some people confuse what I try to do with presenting a *new formula for success*. After all, the HIT model that I present in this book looks quite similar to many of those magic formulas. But in truth, I find it quite embarrassing when that happens. Because the key message I am trying to convey is, in fact, the exact opposite.

My key message is that there will never be a universal recipe for effective collaboration. Of course, I know there are lots of scientific studies about how teams can work together effectively. In the studies I read, I counted hundreds of variables that were proven to influence effective collaboration. Variables at the level of the individual, the team, the organization, and beyond.[13] And in practically every study I found a slightly different formula for successful collaboration. So I find myself sitting on my porch, staring into the shadow of that huge mountain of scientific studies on teamwork, and I can conclude only two things. One, that mountain is far too high for a single person to climb. Two, there is no universal way to collaborate effectively. There are thousands of ways.

The team that became great didn't start off great.
It LEARNED how to produce extraordinary results.
– PETER SENGE[14]

If you remember only one sentence after reading this book, then let it be this one: 'High Impact Teams discover their unique formula for success by *learning* what works and what doesn't by themselves.' A team is not a machine. Imagine your car broke down in four different places:[15] two tires, the engine, and the brakes. The formula to get your car back on the road again is universal. Have a mechanic repair it at each of these four points. That's it. For a team, the reality is quite different. With a team, the most the 'mechanic' can do is *talk* to the car and its parts. Only the car can fix itself. But more importantly, sometimes you have to start repairing the car by fixing its steering wheel. Once that is done, the engine magically starts running again and the tires inflate themselves. In other cases, the engine gets fixed and magically the two tires inflate automatically and the steering wheel grows back. The point is: in contrast to cars, teams are living systems. In living systems, the parts influence one another and have the ability to self-heal.

I admit that it sounds like an expert answering a difficult question with the most irritating counter-question ever: What do *you* think? I feel you. I also dislike answers that avoid the question. Answers that actually aren't answers. But don't worry. In this chapter, I offer you a couple of simple, science-based answers to the question of how High Impact Teams can fix their mechanics.

If you can't explain it simply,
you don't understand it well enough.
– ALBERT EINSTEIN[16]

Paul Stinckens, the founder of Unicorn, reminded me about the first step
to take when trying to put a difficult puzzle together. Start with the corners
and the edges![17] Once the framework is there, fitting the rest of the pieces
becomes a lot easier. In the following 11 pages, I spell out the main messages
of this book by laying out the corners and the edges of the puzzle. I describe
the High Impact Teaming model. Not a new universal formula for effective
collaboration. Just a framework exemplifying what effective teams do to
develop their *own* formula for success. But before I present that HIT model,
I'd like to answer two other frequently asked questions. Where does the word
Teaming suddenly come from? And what does *High Impact* actually mean?

FROM TEAM TO TEAMING

On their way home, Harry and his family notice a man lying in the middle
of the road ahead. He is not moving. Harry hits the brakes and hurries to the
trunk of his car to get the warning triangle out. He starts directing traffic
while his wife Kim, who is a nurse, attends to the man and examines his
pulse and breathing. Nothing. She instructs a bystander: *'Call an ambulance!*
This man has no pulse.' She immediately starts CPR. One minute passes. The
situation is being monitored by somebody from the 911 emergency center
through the bystander's phone. At the same time, the call center remains in
close contact with the ambulance that is on its way.

When I say the word *team*, what kind of collective do you instinctively
imagine? Would you think of a collective such as the nurse, her husband, and
the bystander from the example above? Are they a *team* in your opinion?

One definition that is often cited is this: *'A team is a collection of individuals*
who are independent in their tasks, who share responsibility for outcomes, who
see themselves and who are seen by others as an intact social entity embedded in
one or more larger social systems (for example, business unit or corporation) and

who manage their relationships across organizational boundaries.'[18] Kim, Harry, and the other people in the story above do not really match this definition. When we hear the word *team* we think instead of more stereotypical teams, like management teams and sports teams. Teams with members who work almost exclusively in that one team, with low turnover, clear goals, well-defined working methods and a high degree of trust. Teams who most likely work together face-to-face, within the same time-zone, and for the same organization.

But the long-standing dominance of these types of teams seems to be fading. More and more often, people work in several teams at the same time. More and more often, teams rapidly change in composition in order to keep up with the constantly changing situation, clients, goals, and so on. In some teams, the composition changes so often that the team members don't really know one another at the start of their assignment, let alone trust each other. Often, teams don't start off with clear goals or working methods. Today, many teams don't work in the same building but collaborate across the globe through virtual contact alone.

In 2012, Amy Edmondson wrote the book *Teaming.* She coined the term to mark these fundamental changes in the world of collaboration.[19] The word *teaming* shifts the focus from narrow definitions – what teams *are* or *should be* – to what people *do* when they work together as effectively as possible. Teaming is a verb. It is an action that is not just applicable to standard teams, but also to individuals who meet one another for the first time and collaborate *on the fly*. People working together towards results without the formal structures and relational conditions that are typically associated with the traditional concept of *teams*. Airline attendants with different flight crews every day. Teams in operating rooms with a changing combination of surgeons, anesthetists, and nurses for every surgery. Teams who assemble and dissolve again within the time frame of a single operation.

Once, I did a two day team coaching session with the Extended Executive Committee of a large bank. The top managers in this team, who come from all over Europe, meet face-to-face four times a year. They did not have shared targets, and their CEO was reluctant to take a hierarchical stance. It was agreed with the CEO that he would kick off with a short introduction on the goals and the program of the seminar. He gave an inspiring speech about how they were all about to become a real *team* and he cited some of the typical standards. I could feel the disappointment in the room. All these people had packed agendas. Fear of a huge loss of time dripped from the walls of the conference room.

By the time it was my turn, you could have cut the atmosphere with a knife. But it wasn't just the vibe in the room that made me nervous. Just fifteen minutes before the start of the seminar, I had made some last-minute changes to the slides I was about to present. I slipped in some theory on High Impact Teaming. And I completely forgot to align my new message on *teaming* with the CEO. In my opinion, this group of people did not match the classical definition of a team at all.

I had a choice: either skip my slides and build on what the CEO had just said about becoming a real team, or position myself in opposition to the CEO by unexpectedly pushing the concept of Teaming. I took a risk and chose the second option. On my first slide, there was a picture of a management team and a football team, accompanied by the definition of a team. After a short explanation, I moved to the next slide presenting one question: '*Raise your hand if you think this Extended Executive Committee should become a* team *as defined on the previous slide.*' Nobody moved. I looked in the direction of the CEO. Luckily, he could see the humor in the situation. He nodded and gave me a forgiving smile. In the next few minutes, I introduced the concept of Teaming. You cannot imagine the wave of relief that went through the room: '*We can just think about how we will work together more effectively without having to pretend we are going to become a team?*' Correct! Thank you, Amy Edmondson.

The traditional concept of *team* that comes to mind spontaneously can give direction and clarity. But just as often it is a heavy harness that can get in the way of moving towards more effective collaboration. I wrote this book for everyone who wants to play with the efficiency and effectiveness of the way they work together. It doesn't matter if that collaboration looks like a *classical team* or not. If you have a classical team, great! But that is absolutely not a prerequisite for reading this book. By the way, don't forget that *classical teams* are also increasingly confronted with turnover due to dismissals,[20] burnout, and job-hopping or trends like digitalization and *the new way of working*. Can you remember the last time everything ran smoothly, everyone was productive, and you weren't training any replacements or newcomers?

FROM HOT AIR TO HIGH IMPACT

Kurt is an interim manager. His team performs poorly, the atmosphere is not optimal and it is clear to him that something needs to change. He hires a professional team coach who analyzes the situation. There are personal tensions in the team. The conclusion is that the team needs team building. The coach organizes a vote and the majority agrees to a one-night program. In the evening of the first day, the team coach organizes a gin dropping. Some team members have real doubts about whether this is going to change anything, but they engage diplomatically. After a few gins, the atmosphere changes. When they arrive at the target location, some team members start dancing. They have an awesome party. The next day at ten o'clock, the team goes kayaking. In the afternoon, when most team members have recovered from their hangovers, the team coach challenges them to build a bridge, strong enough to hold a minivan, over a small creek. Everyone cooperates successfully. The mood of the team is elated as Kurt drives them across the creek in the minivan. They all feel as if something has really changed.

Do you want to know what I think about this team coach? That he sells hot air. He encourages a mediocre mindset about collaboration: *The team is a goal in itself.'* But if you start from that mindset, mediocrity or low impact is guaranteed. Chances are that you will attach excessive importance to good relationships, democracy, and the atmosphere in the team. Today, there are plenty of scientific studies that show that such team building has no, negative or inferior long-term effects.[21] That kind of team building is often no more than a pleasant pat on the back or a small plaster on an open wound.

A far more effective mindset is this one: *'The team is never a goal in itself. The reason for the existence of any team is not in the team, but outside of it.'*[22] People with that mindset will build teams for the right reasons: (1) Results, (2) Sustainability, (3) Acceptance, and (4) Essence. In consequence, they will do it far more effectively.

Top teams focus on achieving the desired results. They win the finals. They score the hit. They heal the patient. They exceed the expectations of the customer. Teaming means nothing if it does not ultimately lead to results.

You can work as hard and as much as you like to improve the collaboration in your team, but if that does not lead to results, nothing will change. And in the long run, the entire system will fall apart. When that happens, you can loudly proclaim how unfair that is. That you and your team have done *the right thing*. But sometimes the world is a hard and cold chessboard and the winner takes it all.[23] That's a reality best taken into account. I know what it feels like to be in a team that keeps on failing time and time again. The energy of the team is draining, confidence drops, people start scapegoating, differences in vision are magnified, and so on.

You can learn a lot from failure, and some teams manage to bounce back to a higher level. No team, however, survives failing time and time again. Make sure your team achieves results. Nothing is as powerful for High Impact Teaming as impact. Impact is the basis for motivation, trust, and everything that follows. If the desired results are achieved, psychological safety increases, there is more space for win-win thinking, and the team automatically reorganizes when it encounters small hurdles.

In 2005, I had the opportunity to listen to Ignace Van Doorselaere – former Vice President at AB InBev Western Europe, then CEO at Van de Velde, and now CEO at Neuhaus – explaining to his troops what impact meant to him. He compared it to pushing a row of five domino tiles. Suppose you push the first domino over and the second and the third also fall, but the fourth and the fifth remain upright. Did you have an impact? Many people stop after pushing the first domino over. They did their job so they assume that the desired results will follow. Top team members continue until the last domino falls. Only then is there impact. If the last domino doesn't fall, you might just as well have done nothing.[24] And that last domino is almost never located inside the team, but rather outside of the team, with the customer, the client, the patient. What about the results of your team? Does your last domino fall?

Sustainability

Mediocre teams sometimes manage to push over that last domino once – the so-called *one-hit-wonders*. Maybe they had a lucky shot. Maybe they pressured one another for months to arrive at that single shiny outcome. A week later, two colleagues resign and another is at home with burnout. In the long run, it is likely to go from bad to worse. High Impact Teaming is about achieving sustainable results. It is about learning to work together in such a way that the desired results are achieved again and again and again.

Stephen Covey uses Aesop's fable of the goose that laid the golden eggs to explain sustainability. Aesop[25] tells of a farmer whose goose starts laying golden eggs. In the beginning, the farmer is happy that his goose is making him richer every day. But after a while, he becomes impatient and greedy. The farmer decides not to wait for the golden eggs to come one by one. After all, he knows where those eggs come from. They're all in the belly of the goose. He cuts the goose open and that's the end of the story.

The golden eggs symbolize the results of your team. The goose symbolizes everything that gives you and your colleagues the energy and resources to keep achieving those results time and time again: your body, your colleagues, the way you work together, your home situation, and so on. How is your goose doing?

I see many teams laying golden eggs in a way that is not sustainable. They crush themselves, they try to tackle everything at once and keep telling themselves that after this month it really will become more manageable. Team members place high demands on themselves and on one another, the atmosphere becomes strained and conflicts arise. Confidence decreases and everything costs more energy. People feel undervalued for all the work they do. The goose still lays some golden eggs occasionally, but she is exhausted. High Impact Teaming is about developing a good balance between the wellbeing of the goose and the golden eggs in order to achieve results in a sustainable way.

Acceptance

Sometimes I deal with teams who really think highly of themselves. They have the feeling that they are doing extremely well, but if you ask important stakeholders – colleagues, the supervisor, or the customers, to name but a few – they see something completely different. High Impact Teaming is always a matter of perception. It is never just about the *measurable* or *objective* results. It is always a product of the results a team achieves and the subjective acceptance of these results by relevant stakeholders. Jan Van der Vurst summarizes this in his book *Impact*,[26] using the following formula: **I**mpact = **Q**uality × **A**cceptance. Measurable quality of the results can be good, but if the acceptance is zero, then the impact of your team will also be zero.

This formula for impact does not suggest that you always have to go with the flow. It does not say that pleasing stakeholders and self-marketing are more important than intrinsic quality. Top teams also dare to make unpopular decisions and bite into the sour apple. Sometimes they embark on adventures that others think are unfeasible or unrealistic. Sometimes they see the importance of what they do before their environment understands it. But they are aware of the effect that negative perceptions have on the resources the team will receive from its environment. High Impact Teaming is always a matter of perception, but top teams are not slaves to the perceptions of others. Performance evolves fairly steadily, but acceptance can fluctuate greatly. The perceptions of customers, shareholders, employees and the like are fluctuating like the stock exchange. Sometimes they suddenly go up or down a hundred points. High Impact Teaming is not about responding to every rumor like a headless chicken; quite the contrary. Top teams go for quality, but they are aware of the importance of perceptions and always manage to get acceptance in the end.

Essence

For some people, winning again and again, and getting the credit for it is already more than enough. But most people want more. They want to do something that matters. They want to find fulfillment by dealing with something that matters to them: essence. Of course, what essence is differs from person to person, but no one seems to find essence in polishing the underside of the banister day after day.[27]

I remember a top manager who realized at the age of 55 that he had achieved so many great results with his teams, but that he actually didn't give a hoot about that. That looking back he would rather have continued working as an engineer. He preferred uncovering real practical solutions and diving into the technical details. It was the best time of his life. What does *High Impact Teaming* mean if you ignore that?

How do you find out whether you are doing essential things in and with your team? First of all, it makes sense to listen to the people in your environment. Do they think that you are doing something important? But equally important: have the guts to sit on your cloud once in a while. Take some distance, and dare to ask yourself some uncomfortable questions. Listen to your true voice and the authentic voices of the people around you:

-   Do you do something that really fulfills you? And here I am not referring to filling your wardrobe and bank accounts, but to filling your soul.
-   How do you evaluate this team when you judge it against your deepest and most personal values?
-   What would others think about you and this team if they really knew everything about what you are doing, including the dark side?
-   What impact on the world do you have with your team today and what impact would you be able or willing to have?

THE EDGES AND CORNERS

High Impact Teaming leads to impactful and sustainable results, acceptance, and essence. Great, but how can you do it? How can you get there? The High Impact Teaming model that I present below will help you see clearly why your team is doing well or what is holding it back. It will help you to tackle opportunities and barriers more effectively. I created the HIT model by dividing the mountain of variables that have proved to influence team effectiveness in scientific literature into six interconnected areas: Team Learning, Visioning, Organizing, Safe Teaming, Individual Impact, and Context. Of course, not all variables are covered and integrated. But that wasn't my ambition. I just wanted to create a structure that covers the key areas in which top teams work and the key activities they perform to discover their own formula for success. So again, not a new formula for team success. Just a tool to frame and simplify the endless chaos of possibilities.

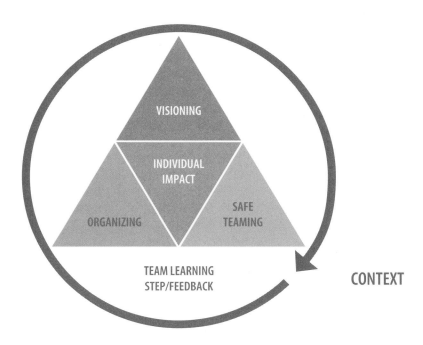

Three groups of variables at the team level form the core of the HIT model and this book: **Visioning** (Chapter 4), **Organizing** (Chapter 5) and **Safe Teaming** (Chapter 3). These are the three corners of the puzzle. Imagine you are part of a team of explorers aboard a small rowing boat searching for the holy grail.

Visioning helps the crew develop a shared vision of where exactly they want to sail to and why. Shared vision gives the team direction, the route and, especially, energy. But the shared vision can only be put into practice by systems and people – the boat and the crew. *Organizing* is about making the boat sail as efficiently as possible, by finding, developing and deploying better systems, structures and routines. For example, you can increase the width of the blade of your oar to increase the impact you exert on the water in order to sail faster. You can also agree on a division of roles with rowers, a captain, and a drummer to create rhythm and predictability. *Safe Teaming* is the art of increasing the psychological safety in the team. That is why your crew needs to show vulnerability and to speak openly and honestly. It increases the likelihood that you will get to learn who has what opinion and who wants to do what. Team psychological safety is important if you want to make sure you know whether your colleagues are really sitting in the boat and when someone is about to fall overboard.

In expedition teams, there is one thing you know for sure: the situation of the team changes constantly.[28] Suddenly, the wind changes because there's a storm on the way. After a while, the ship that you once considered state of the art is now seen as a piece of junk. But the situation in the team is also constantly evolving. At a certain moment your team discovers that the military map you were using is incorrect and the boat is heading in the wrong direction; that the systems fail and cost energy instead of saving energy; or that all sorts of things are happening under the waterline, quietly eroding the psychological safety. At those moments Visioning, Organizing, or Safe Teaming can suddenly become crucial to refresh the effectiveness of the team.

> *Nobody can go back and start a new beginning, but anyone can start today and make a new ending.*
> – JAMES R. SHERMAN[29]

Visioning, Organizing, and Safe Teaming are all forms of **Team Learning** (see Chapter 2). They are examples of what teams can do to refresh themselves, their vision, their organization, and culture; and to adapt to external or internal changes. High Impact Teams learn by slowing down to go faster. Peter Senge was the first to give the concept *team learning* international attention, with his now world-famous best seller, *The Fifth Discipline*. Since that book was published in 1990, empirical research on team learning has increased enormously. Time and time again, researchers came to the same conclusion: team learning leads to team effectiveness.[30] It is what teams do to discover their own formula for success. Generally, they do it in two distinct ways: STEP (Stop-Think-Evaluate-Proceed) and Feedback.

Last but not least, there are two other crucial groups of variables in the HIT model. Two other groups of variables that influence how teams learn: the ship's crew and the water in which it sails. On the one hand, there are all sorts of variables that have to do with **Individual Impact** (Chapter 6): habits, mindsets, roles and so on. They form the basis for everything that happens in the team, including the speed and quality of team learning. On the other hand, there are all sorts of variables that have to do with why and how teams do or do not learn effectively in and from their **Context** (Chapter 7).[31] The purpose of the team is not inside of it. It is in its context. Hence, High Impact Teaming means nothing unless teams learn from their context to have sustainable impact in their context.

A final component of this HIT model is not visible in my drawing of the model: **Trust** (Chapter 8). I discuss Trust in detail in the last chapter. Trust is crucial for High Impact Teaming, because there is only one certainty in teams: you know nothing for sure. You are not sure whether or not the other team members really want to go in the same direction; whether or not they will really adhere to the agreements made; whether or not they will respond well when you show who you really are; whether or not the energy that you invest in team learning will actually lead to constructive changes and thus generate more energy. You cannot start without the belief that team learning makes sense. Trust is the oil in the HIT gearbox: without oil, progress requires unnecessary energy, everything goes much more slowly, and eventually your motor breaks. Trust is sometimes presented as a crucial piece of the puzzle. But that's not how I see it: for me, Trust is the glue that binds the pieces of the puzzle together.

The only true wisdom is in knowing you know nothing.
     – SOCRATES[32]

CHAPTER 2
TEAM LEARNING – STEP & FEEDBACK

The eight-member top management team of an organization with more than 10,000 employees has been performing well in recent years. The organization has grown considerably. But the wave of growth on which the team has been riding has now been broken and the pressure has increased. The past few months have been very hectic – so hectic that for weeks the team has not found a single moment to really stand still, face the problems together, and come up with solutions. The tank of the car is nearly empty, but everyone feels that there is just no time to stop and refuel.

The CEO, Kirsten, asked me to observe her team and give feedback during a two-day strategy summit. She kicked off the offsite program herself with a short speech about the *why* of the summit. *'... In short, for me it's mainly about refueling as much as possible. Take the time to think together about our direction and strategy. But also take time to reflect on the way we work together, to give each other feedback, and to listen to how each of us is sitting in the boat.'*

We agreed that after her opening speech I would briefly explain how I would guide and observe them during the following days. I explained I was there to shadow the team and would of course treat the content of their conversations confidentially. I promised not to intervene during their meetings, but to write down my thoughts. During the afternoon of day two, I would share my observations. Then we would collectively reflect on the way the team was working together. To finish, I had two more slides to explain what I would pay attention to.

Team learning: STEP & Feedback. Slide 1. Click.

'Imagine that the people in this cartoon have been instructed by Kirsten to reach
the top of the tree as quickly as possible. What would you recommend them to
do?'[33]

Wally, the sales director, laughed as he shouted: 'Climb faster!'

Two others: 'Take the elevator!'

I jumped in: 'I would advise them to stop for a moment, walk around the tree
twice and then, to do whatever they think is best. Research shows that effective
teams do that regularly. They manage to slow down to go faster. Usually they
do it briefly, winning some percentages, but at crucial moments they are able
to make 180 degree turns as well. A meta-analysis by Sanner and Bunderson
shows a population correlation between team learning and team performance
of 39 percent.'[34]

'But we don't have time for that! Climb faster, damn it!' Kirsten said with a teasing smile. *'Do you have any idea how many trees there are in the forest?'* I waited quietly for the laughter after Kirsten's joke to subside and continued my second and final slide.

'Slowing down to go faster is a fancy way to describe how teams learn to improve their performance and impact. It is not about going on a two-day offsite for every problem you encounter. Effective teams manage to repair the airplane while airborne, not only when it's on the ground. They are able to replace the engines of the plane during the flight, while the passengers are complaining about the cookies. They manage to learn on the fly – in and between meetings. You can basically engage in effective team learning in two different ways. On the one hand, by continuously seeking and giving open and honest feedback and by really being open to receive it. One-on-one, in team, and from all your internal and external stakeholders. But Kirsten told me that feedback is a piece of cake for this team, so I don't think I need to go into it. On the other hand, team learning is about doing a team STEP once in a while. I think it is possible to summarize almost everything there is to know about team learning in that four-letter word: STEP. Stop, Think, Evaluate, Proceed.'

I took my time to explain exactly what STEP means. People are not machines. Sometimes we get overwhelmed and we do something without thinking. It's human to react. Do you know the feeling? When you impulsively respond to an email that annoys you? Stimulus ... Rakatakatak ... response! And less than a second later, you realize you should not have done it. That it was not aligned with your personal values. This phenomenon is what Stephen Covey[35] referred to as *reactivity* in his book *The Seven Habits*. Stimulus – don't think – response. On an individual level, STEP is about using your fundamental freedom of choice to stay in control of your own behavior, instead of reacting impulsively. Effective team members don't just jump from stimulus to response. At important moments, they use the power of self-awareness to recognize how they feel, calm down emotionally, slow down physically, and focus mentally. **Stop**. They take some distance and use this distance to see more possibilities. Using the power of imagination, they think outside of the box and see more than one or two possible responses. **Think**. Based on their vision, values and beliefs they make a choice between the different alternatives. They use the power of their conscience to choose the right option. **Evaluate**. Finally, they use the power of will to actually implement the choice they made and to take responsibility for its consequences. **Proceed**.

Time and time again, teams fall into the same trap. Under pressure, they switch to reactive mode. They make decisions on autopilot without checking them against their vision and conscience, often based on the conviction that there is no other way to move forward. That there is just one course of action. That there is no time to ... STEP at the team level is the beating heart of High Impact Teaming. It's about slowing down together to move on in greater alignment, in meetings and between meetings. It starts with someone who dares to stop and convince the team to take a step back together. **Stop**. Team members chart the territory of the problem together and share all kinds of out of the box solutions. Both finished and unfinished ideas are put on the table. They really listen to one another. And they dare to ask questions in order to get ideas to the surface that are not shared spontaneously. **Think**. They engage in good fights to arrive at a shared conclusion based on their conscience, their values and the broader picture. **Evaluate**. They set up a system to ensure that they will actually put into practice what they decided together. **Proceed**.

High Impact Teams regularly take STEPs on a task level. This helps them to solve specific problems collaboratively, to iterate a certain product, or to push a strategic priority forward. But they also engage in STEPs about how they work together as a team or about how they can tackle interpersonal issues.[36]

'Summarized in one sentence,' I concluded, *'during the next two days I will observe how you learn as a team, how you give each other feedback, and how you STEP together.'* My presentation was finished. Some team members looked at me with a slightly indignant expression. I had the feeling that some were a bit frustrated that I had bothered them with such simple things. There were so many complex and urgent things waiting for them! They went straight to work. I sat myself down in the corner of the room with a small notebook and recorded everything I saw.

The next day after lunch, it was time for the debriefing. I had observed a number of very intensive meetings during the past one and a half days. The team was exhausted. But did they really take a step back together? Nope. Nada. Nothing. At least, that was my perception. I was nervous. I observed eight individuals who had done nothing but speed up, with their noses to the grindstone. But I also knew that in their perception they had done a great job. After all, they had hardly discussed any operational details for a day and a half!

At this level, entering a debriefing to teach people some lessons really doesn't work. I took a marker and made two columns on the flipchart. One with a plus sign and one with an arrow pointing up. The instruction was simple: *'Do an analysis of how you worked together as a team during the past two days. What worked? What improvements can be made? At the end, choose three key improvement points and decide together what you will do with them.'* Kirsten took the initiative to facilitate the discussion, which turned out to be a pretty hard job. Ideas were flying around. The team members hopped from one topic to another. They talked and talked without really listening to one another. A very similar pattern to all the meetings I had observed during the past day and a half. I crossed my arms, leaned back and watched them fall back into old habits. Except for a few points, their analysis was accurate, but the essence was wrong. They did admit that they had only given one another feedback on the results achieved or the *what* and that it would actually be a good idea to occasionally address *how* they do things. But they put STEP on the side of the positive points. *'We did this STEP thing really well during the past couple of days!'*

Eighteen minutes into the discussion, they had already filled two pages of the flipchart, but none of the points was really analyzed in depth. They pretended to understand one another, but I felt that that wasn't really the case. Their debriefing was coming to an end as they tried to decide on the priorities. Again, four out of eight people were talking at the same time. Now was my moment to intervene. *'Even now, at this very moment, you are not listening to one another.'* Kirsten's team fell silent and their heads turned in my direction. I immediately felt that half the group was on board with my statement. Although I was sure that everyone somehow knew that they often interrupted one another, I was by no means certain that I would be able to make my point. *'You're claiming that you really did a lot of good STEPs. Do you know how often I jotted down a qualitative STEP in my notebook?'* Silence. *'Not once.'* Now I had everyone's attention.

Would you like to know how this debriefing ended? In the following paragraphs of this chapter, I use this case as an example to elaborate further on the DNA of High Impact Teaming: Team learning. After a brief introduction to the Team Learning concept, I will zoom in on the two things that High Impact Teams do in order to boost team effectiveness: STEP and feedback.

WHAT IS TEAM LEARNING?

Can teams learn? Teams don't have a brain in which they store things and recall them later, do they?! Individuals have brains. Individuals learn. You could even say that they are constantly learning. Not always consciously, but every experience changes something. It leaves a trace. Sometimes those traces disappear very quickly, sometimes they remain visible a bit longer, but it is impossible not to learn. Teams also learn. All the time. Because teams consist of individuals who are constantly learning. They develop new ideas, visions, products, ways of working, habits. But just as with individuals, teams do not always learn effectively.

So there are teams that invest energy in team learning and don't become more effective? Of course! But let's be clear; on average, there is a very strong positive correlation between team learning and team effectiveness.[37] It makes sense. We live in a time where the environment is constantly changing and the same laws apply to teams as to all other living organisms: $S = f\,(L \geq E)$. The chances of **S**urvival depend on the extent to which **L**earning is greater than or equal to changes in the **E**nvironment.[38] But be aware, scientific research almost always reports averages, and sometimes even averages of averages.[39] If teams learn at the wrong moments or in the wrong ways, team learning can also impair the effectiveness of the team. In the following paragraphs, I will explain in a nutshell what team learning is, and how you can do it effectively.

Team learning occurs when *individuals change something* in the way they *think and act as a team* or in the *collective products or results* that reflect that change. Since learning has a positive connotation for most people, I will usually only refer to it as team learning when a team does so with the intention or with the effect of *improvement*.

There is no one simple model or definition of team learning that integrates all facets. I can tell: I made an attempt to grasp the complexity of the concept during one of my doctorates (see the figure below),[40] but that attempt was not entirely successful. Why not? Because I didn't grasp the complexity. I just shoved it down the throats of my scientific readers.

There are so many different models and definitions that it is quite difficult to reach a single integrated definition of team learning. Sometimes team learning is about an improvement of one percentage, sometimes it is about a radical shift. Sometimes it happens by chance, sometimes intentionally. Sometimes a team learns by doing something a lot, sometimes it learns by talking about something. Sometimes the results of team learning are hardly visible, sometimes team learning leads to very concrete and visible outcomes.

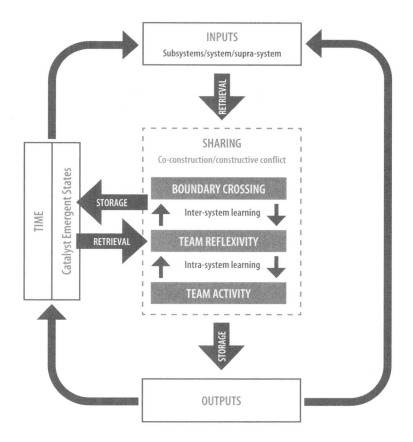

The number of ways to describe team learning reflects the number of ways teams learn. But there are two classifications that are used so often that I definitely want to share them with you. Karen Jehn and Joyce Rupert[41] describe three different levels at which teams learn based on the *topic* of learning. Sometimes they learn at several of those levels at the same time, sometimes very clearly at only one of the three:

- **The task:** learning about the *content* of the job, professional knowledge and competences, the direction of the team, the products it creates, the services it provides, the results, et cetera;
- **The process:** learning about the *way* the team works, roles and responsibilities, team routines, work procedures, et cetera;
- **The interpersonal:** learning about *who* is in the team and how to interpret each other's behavior in the context of their personal life, personality, history, family, et cetera.

Another classification was developed by Valerie Sessa and Manuel London.[42] They describe three different levels at which teams learn based on the *way* they learn and what *caused* them to learn:

- **Adaptive team learning:** when teams respond to external incentives and feedback by making incremental adjustments to achieve the goal in a more efficient or faster way;
- **Generative team learning:** when teams proactively learn, develop, change, or explore skills, knowledge, behaviors, and interaction patterns to improve team performance;
- **Transformative team learning:** when, after a moment of disorientation, teams fundamentally adjust their sense, purpose, strategy, or structure, or change another core element in the group.

To keep it simple, I summarize Team Learning as STEP and feedback. STEP at the team level, feedback at the team level or between individuals. I realize that in this way, I am drastically simplifying the concept. Nevertheless, this simple and practical framework provides enough room to deal with every important process variable in team learning research. Below I zoom in on what STEP and feedback can mean for you.

STEP is a meta-habit of highly effective teams. Not only do they regularly take time for a planned big STEP, for example by organizing a more extensive evaluation moment, but they also constantly engage in unplanned baby STEPs. For example, they take fifteen minutes during a meeting to step back and adjust the direction of the team, or they take a few minutes during an action to fine-tune the way they are doing something. They do it regularly. It's a habit.

Ineffective teams also use STEP, but they deploy it in a more linear way: they wait until they have no other choice left but to learn. When they are stuck somewhere halfway up the tree and are too tired to keep climbing. Why? Two reasons. On the one hand, they think – often with good reason – that stopping and sitting together for the *umpteenth* meeting will cost them an enormous amount of energy and won't take them forward. Lots of *blah blah* and little or no *boom boom*. They prove themselves right by lowering the quality of their STEP moments to the point that they are no longer about slowing down to go faster, but about slowing down to go even slower. On the other hand, learning in those teams often has a very negative, almost depressing connotation: bad grades, looking for someone to blame, punishment, proving that we cannot do it, and so on. This is extremely problematic because STEP is not just a rational series of activities, there is a large *emotional* component too. It is not just about co-creating the right idea and then executing it. It is just as much about co-creating a shared willingness to go for it and the feeling that the team is able to make it happen. It is therefore crucial to frame STEP moments as constructively and positively as possible[43] – as moments that generate a positive desire to improve, and a positive belief that the team is able to do so. If you don't succeed, people in your team will quickly lose interest in jumping onto the High Impact Teaming boat. Trust and positive energy are the basic fuel of effective STEP moments.

Based on my debriefing with Kirsten's team, I describe what it means to go through the four stages of STEP in a way that gives more energy than it costs.

STOP

I got up, took the marker from Kirsten and turned over the scribbled piece of paper. On an empty flipchart sheet, I wrote down the four-letter acronym STEP in capital letters, circled the letter S – referring to Stop – and asked:

'*Did you stop?*'

Marc reacted, slightly irritated: '*We are here, aren't we?*'

'*Have you stopped, right now at this very moment?*' I repeated.

Kirsten understood perfectly what I meant.

'*Even when I explicitly set the framework to stop for an hour to look at things from a distance, you keep on running the race in your head. Stop is not just about sitting around a table together. The essence of Stop is that you lower the adrenaline in the team to a level where everyone is able to take some distance and think together. You are like a train that keeps on going. At this moment, at least two people are still mentally in the previous meeting and at least one person is preparing for the next one. Elise, you are preoccupied with your smartphone half the time. No idea what that is about. I don't care. But has this team stopped? I don't think so.*'

Team learning starts with self-awareness. We often fail to stop as a team because we don't realize that we are racing. We think we have stopped, but that's not really the case. Even though the team members have managed to physically come together in the same room to talk about important topics, this does not mean the team has stopped. As long as the adrenaline has not dropped sufficiently to really detach mentally and emotionally, to sit on your cloud together and start a real conversation, the team has not stopped.

On one hand, stopping requires the team to lower the pressure to a level where team members can focus mentally. Without this mental focus, team members fail to think and listen effectively. The discussion goes nowhere, jumping from one point to the next without finishing anything. On the other hand, there is also an important emotional component. Sometimes the energy is not too high, but just too negative or too positive for an effective STEP. When the mood is too negative, team members only spot the problems. They fail to come up with solutions in which they can actually believe. When the mood is too positive, team members become over-confident. They are less able to spot problems and don't actually feel the need to STEP.

There is no magic formula for stopping teams. I advocate mindfulness and meditation for team members to learn how to focus mentally, but I'm quite sure that while it will work in some teams, it will flop in others. The only constant is that stopping a team when it most needs to STEP requires courage. Of course, it is easy to say *stop* to a team when you are the leader or when you have the solution. It is in line with the traditional vision of leadership: the leader's job is to stop the team and tell the team members what needs to be done. Stopping a team when you do *not* have the solution or when you are not the formal leader is a lot more difficult. Everyone is so preoccupied that you really need to stand strong in order to stop all the adrenaline junkies. In many places, doing that could be considered as slowing down to slow down: seeking attention, an act of resistance, and so on.

What you need in those cases is *I Don't Know Leadership:*[44] the art of making contact with your deepest feelings and using them as a basis to decide that something is wrong. This type of leadership is about daring to be vulnerable and to say: '*I don't know what the solution is, but I want us to stop. Help me to come up with the solution.*'

THINK

> '*What does it mean to think together at the team level?*' I asked. '*Thinking out of the box,*' Elise said. '*Sharing and capturing ideas,*' said Kirsten. '*That's correct. But even when something is written on a flipchart, this does not mean that it is shared. If nobody listens, there is no sharing. Moreover, there are three people in this room who have not said a word in the last 20 minutes. But we think that's okay. The same way we think it is okay during our meetings. Nobody asks what they think to get their ideas on the table. We assume that if you don't say something – at this level – you have nothing valuable to say. Period.*'

Once your team stops, you have a chance to come to a more qualitative level of thinking together. But that is easier said than done: *thinking* appears to be one of the most difficult things to do as a team. The most common problems in the Think phase are these: teams jump to the first conclusion, they think within the lines of realistic and acceptable solutions, they lapse into the habit of complaining and nagging, they leave taboos under the table, they don't listen to one another, they mistakenly assume they understand one another, and so on.

After the team has stopped, it is very tempting to fall into the trap of jumping straight to the conclusion. People don't like uncertainty or a lack of clarity. We use our thinking ability to create clarity in the chaos around us. But if you let the urge for clarity prevail over the need for effective solutions, there is little chance that you will really use the learning potential of your team. Teams only start learning effectively if they take a generous amount of time to share out-of-the-box ideas. High Impact Teams start from the mindset that there is never just one perspective or one option. Even if the conclusion is obvious, they will still try to bring other perspectives to the surface.

Another reason the Think phase sometimes fails is that the whole team ends up complaining and nagging. A lot of stories and ideas are shared, but they are all about what others need to change. The team behaves as if it is the victim of circumstances. It doesn't see where it can improve itself to have an impact on the situation. The longer the team stays in this complaining mode, the less time it has to focus on what it can change. Help the team to refocus on what it can influence. Once the team succeeds in charting the territory of the problem within its own circle of influence, the energy will shift completely. Suddenly, team members will start coming up with all kinds of alternatives they can actually influence themselves. If not, the entire STEP moment will have no impact whatsoever and will leave a bad taste in your mouth.

Another possible reason for failing at the Think phase is that there are taboos in the team and nobody wants to take the risk of putting them on the table. We avoid certain topics or ideas because we are afraid of addressing them. We are afraid of what will happen when we open Pandora's box. That is why we neatly color between the lines of what is acceptable and desirable or what we think is acceptable and desirable for others. Unfortunately, none of these behaviors leads to an effective Think.

A final problem that I often encounter is this strange phenomenon: everyone thinks sharing is taking place, but no one is really listening. Even people who say they are listening are not necessarily listening. They try to listen, but hear only the information that fits their reasoning. *Confirmation bias* is the academic term for this phenomenon. From the moment you think your own idea is pretty clever, you start looking for confirmation in what others say. In consequence, you detect only elements that match your idea. It is often easy to find at least a dozen examples of team members who ignore each other, overrule others, talk at the same time, fail to ask questions, fail to build on the input of other team members, misinterpret one another, and so on. But there is one crucial law in teams: if team members don't listen to one another, there is no real sharing and therefore no real thinking as a team. Sharing is at least as much about listening as it is about talking.

For me, listening is not just about keeping quiet and taking it in. It is also about asking open-ended questions to elicit ideas from people who don't spontaneously share their thoughts. How often have you seen teams who think they share information with one another, but ignore the fact that almost half of them have not said a word? Why is it that we don't keep on questioning one another until we get the best idea out of the team? One of the reasons is that we are swift to assume that we understand each other.[45] Sometimes it is a good idea to check, even when it all seems obvious. An effective Think phase means that the team dares to put all relevant ideas on the table. It means you dare to share ideas that are not yet complete. But it also means that you dare to ask your silent colleagues what they think. A simple 'Does everyone agree?' is sometimes not enough; you may need to ask 'What do you think?' to get everyone involved.

Then, I would like to make one final comment. Some teams have a poor Think phase because they simply don't have enough ideas or their ideas are just not good enough. If it's not in the team, it won't come out in a STEP moment. STEP is not a magical solution for everything. Sometimes teams overestimate their own potential or underestimate all the interesting things happening outside of the team. High Impact Teaming is also about the habit of looking outside. Even if you think your own solutions are fantastic, you can still benefit from acquiring resources, feedback and knowledge from outside the team. In the academic literature, this is called *boundary crossing*.[46] You can read more about boundary crossing in Chapter 7.

EVALUATE

'Evaluate. You guys evaluate in the easiest way possible: by being very kind to each other and following the highest in rank. Half of what's on the flipchart are Kirsten's words. No offense, Kirsten. But your team has never started a good fight or engaged in constructive conflict. At the point where you started choosing priorities, the evaluation system became even more simplistic. You all talk about the issue and the last thing said is considered the choice of the team. But do you really weigh the different options against your vision? Do you really confront each other? Marc and John, I think you do not entirely agree with the fact that the first point has been chosen as a priority. Am I right?'

They both nodded. Kirsten frowned. *'What? But you were both here when we decided that, right? Why didn't you say something?'* Marc answered, almost whispering. *'There is no point in mentioning it ...'* Everyone, except Kirsten, understood perfectly what he meant. The way the debriefing ended is irrelevant here, but I can tell you one thing: it lasted far longer than planned.

After an effective Think phase, there are usually a lot of ideas on the table that need to be evaluated in order to reach a shared decision. But the people in the team have different opinions about these ideas, so sometimes they get stuck in the discussion. There are three standard scenarios that demonstrate how Low Impact Teams solve such situations. In task-oriented teams, team members tend to follow what the expert, the highest in rank, or the loudest person keeps repeating. Relationship-oriented teams usually find salvation in the voting phenomenon: *'Two people want to go to the left, three people want to go to the right? Right it is!'* The third scenario goes as follows: team members fire one option after the other at each other. Nobody really listens to what the other team members are saying. And the option that was fired last gets chosen, almost by accident, because there is no time left.

These three options are all very easy and superficial ways to make a decision. At best, they are emergency solutions in times of crisis. Teams that run on dominance, democracy, or coincidence usually make stupid decisions compared to the decisions the individuals in the team would come up with. They do not harvest the diversity in the team. Dominance, democracy, or coincidence are symptoms of one and the same disease: the inability to engage in constructive conflicts as a team in order to evaluate effectively. The reason is simple: people don't engage in the discussion because they are afraid of destructive conflicts.

What matters most in the evaluation phase is that you replace *no fights* or *bad fights* with *good fights*. A *bad fight* is a conflict in which different points of view emerge, but the team blocks them or becomes dysfunctional because emotions and egos take the upper hand. The communication deteriorates or even stops and there is no shared conclusion. In a *good fight*, the different points of view are put on the table, but instead of stopping communication, it leads to a deepening of the communication. The conversation does not die at the level of individual opinions. Teams that engage in *good fights* ask questions like *'What is your interest behind the thing you want?'*, *'Why do you think this or that?'* Or counter with *'I do not agree, because of this and that.'* A *good fight* always ends with some kind of – at least temporary – conclusion that all parties can agree on.[47] Every team that successfully engages in constructive conflicts has invented its own framework – process and rules – to have fights in a constructive way. That framework explains part of the difference between a good or a bad fight. A ring, gloves, a mouthpiece, and a number of clear agreements help to organize an effective *good fight*. If those are not in place, the chances of ending up in a street fight are higher.

Teams that succeed in creating good fights usually do not come up with insights or decisions that are supported by just one person or even by the majority of the team. They come up with something that – at least at the time of the decision – everyone in the team supports. They do not evaluate on the basis of power, vote, or coincidence, but on the basis of vision, conscience and values – and as such, on the basis of the best in themselves.

'Yes, but if we involve everyone in every decision and give them the opportunity to have an opinion, we will remain stuck in eternal discussions and we will never come to a decision,' Kirsten comments. She is right. Sometimes everyone immediately agrees 100 percent. Then of course there is no need for an in-depth discussion. And there are also situations that simply do not lend themselves to long discussions. Think of the fire brigade facing a house in flames. At that point, organizing an hour of discussions about the plan action is not appropriate. Sometimes leadership is about taking quick decisions and acting. Pushing people to the exit. They will forgive you for the rudeness in the process and be grateful for the outcome once they are outside the burning building. It is true that some teams exhaust themselves with endless good fights. They think that they are good at STEP because they keep discussions going with each other. The philosophers. This is what I refer to as slowing down to slow down. Effective teams know that they can only reduce their workload by keeping the Evaluation phase sober and efficient.

Some teams block in the Evaluation phase because there are no decisive arguments. And when the meeting comes to an end, they postpone the point to the next meeting as they fear making a wrong decision. These teams have the mindset that teams can only learn by doing things right. But a more effective mindset is that teams can also learn by making mistakes: *fail fast forward*.[48] A quote that is incorrectly ascribed to both Winston Churchill and Abraham Lincoln is a great summary of this idea: *'Success is stumbling from failure to failure without loss of enthusiasm.'*[49] When the difference in options is close to zero, High Impact Teams sometimes dare to make a decision based on 51 percent certainty and just try it out. They make a clear hypothesis based on their framework and test it during a defined period of time. They dare to engage in experiments. While experimenting, their goal is not to prove that they are right, but instead to prove that they are wrong. Mediocre teams prefer 110 percent certainty first and then want to prove that they made the right choice, even if that requires ignoring and distorting ridiculous amounts of information. They walk around in Boston with a map of New York and keep looking for the Empire State Building to prove that their map is the right one. There it is again, that damn confirmation bias.

PROCEED

Four frogs are sitting on the edge of the lake. Together they decide that the fattest frog should jump into the lake first. How many frogs are sitting at the edge of the lake now? Four. Making a team decision does not guarantee execution at all. Proceed is about closing the gap between decision and action. Mentally, Proceed is about knowing what to do. The quality of the mental Proceed depends on the ability to make decisions concrete. Emotionally, Proceed is about closure of the past and desire for the future. It requires the ability to let go of any disputes that came up during the discussion and to move forward together. It requires the belief that this STEP moment was truthful and useful and that it will contribute to the effectiveness of the team. Last but not least, it requires the desire to execute what has been agreed upon, and the responsibility to keep others accountable when they don't show the discipline to execute.

To properly explain the Proceed phase, it might be helpful to give an example of what happens when things go wrong in this phase. Imagine you have spent an entire meeting with the team, focused on how you can solve a particular problem. You brainstormed, listened to one another, and made decisions together. The meeting is over and what do you see? Nothing happens. Everyone just keeps on doing what they had planned to do in the first place. And above all, they don't keep each other accountable ... What went wrong? It is very likely that the Stop, Think and Evaluate phases were not as qualitative as you had hoped. But sometimes things just go wrong in the Proceed phase itself.

In effective teams, concrete decisions are made and they are converted from *declarations of intent* to *implementation plans*. Specific agreements with a clear who, what, how, when, et cetera. A check is made as to whether everyone agrees mentally and wants to proceed together emotionally. It's not just about finding a solution and getting it done, but also about feeling motivated to move on. STEP is about investing energy to create more energy. But it is also about getting things done. A team member is assigned the responsibility or a system is set up to ensure that it actually happens. The Proceed phase involves the discipline of individual team members to implement the team decisions. But it is also about creating the framework to hold each other accountable, and giving each other feedback or support when agreements are not fulfilled.

If you learn something as an individual, it goes something like this. You store information via your short-term memory in your long-term memory. You do this in a relatively structured way, which enables you to recall the stored information at a later stage. As a matter of fact, it is impossible to convince your environment that you have actually learned something if you are unable to recall what you have saved. Saving alone is never enough. However, teams sometimes ignore the importance of retrieval in the Proceed phase. We seem to unconsciously believe that saving alone is enough. We save things without even wondering how or when we will recall that knowledge or implement the action.

Storage and retrieval[50] are just as crucial at the team level. A lot of energy is lost because decisions are not implemented, written reports are never used, or because information is not stored in a way that lends itself to being recalled at the right time. An effective Proceed phase is crucial to ensure that the energy you invest in team learning pays off.

WARNING!

STEP is not a methodology. It's not a four-item checklist for your meetings. Copy-pasting STEP into your own team will probably not work. Rather than a methodology, think of STEP as a philosophy. Something to implement in your own way. Considering it as a philosophy gives you the freedom to make it your own. But it also enables you to adopt STEP within the framework you already use today (PDCA, scrum, Kanban, Six Sigma, etc.) and improve its impact. Teams that copy-paste STEP blame the method when it doesn't work. High Impact Teams succeed in implementing STEP as a philosophy, and keep on adjusting it to their team until it works.

And even then, STEP doesn't always work like a dream. Although we describe STEP as a sequence of four phases, it shouldn't be interpreted as strictly sequential. Rather, teams need the flexibility to go back and forth until they feel that their decision and agreements are an answer to the right question. Sometimes, it's only when you arrive at the Evaluate phase that you realize you were discussing the wrong question, not all options surfaced, et cetera. No use going further – back to Stop.

THE POWER OF A FEEDBACK CULTURE

STEP is one of the two crucial engines of High Impact Teaming. The other one is feedback. In effective teams, both engines reinforce each other continuously.

> *Without feedback, a group can change,*
> *but cannot learn.*
> *– MANUEL LONDON & VALERIE I. SESSA[51]*

Catherine Gabelica integrated the fragmented research on feedback in team settings.[52] She describes feedback as the process during which *team members* or *people outside of the team* openly and honestly share perceptions and suggestions with team members.[53] On the one hand, this concerns feedback from *outside* the team. High Impact Teams are constantly looking for unfiltered feedback from their environment. They understand that the *raison d'être* of the team is not to be found in the team, but outside of it. They realize that without feedback from their environment, the team is like a car with blinded windows. If you want to know more about the importance of feedback for adapting to your context, refer to Chapter 7. On the other hand, this process concerns feedback shared *within* the team. Without direct feedback, team members don't receive any information about their own results or behaviors. Without this information, they won't be able to adjust their behavior in a way that could help the team. Your colleagues often have a clear opinion about what you're doing well and what can be improved. But that does not necessarily mean they will say it. Without a healthy feedback culture, team effectiveness will decrease because it blocks the entire team learning engine. Frictions and frustrations grow below the waterline. Team members don't share concerns and solutions during STEP moments. People are not doing what they promised, but nobody is keeping them accountable ...[54]

Some people feel dizzy as soon as they hear a fuzzy word like *feedback culture*. But in fact, cultures have a very concrete and tangible component: habits. In the end, culture is just the sum of your habits. In a feedback culture, people have the habit of giving each other feedback, asking for feedback, and being open to it. Team members in Low Impact Teams rarely give each other effective feedback. If it happens, it is probably the manager who gives feedback to his/her subordinates. This feedback is usually limited to things that are not going well, and very oriented towards the *what* or the results. Team members perceive feedback as an assessment of their performance (remember the grades we got at school? *#assessmentoflearning*).[55] In effective teams, no one waits for the official moments to give feedback. Feedback happens now, when it has the biggest effect on the learning and performance of the team[56] *#flashfeedback*[57]. On the spot, during the match, in action, one-on-one and in team, in the meetings and in between meetings. In High Impact Teams, team members also give their supervisor feedback. The feedback is not only about things that are not working, but also about what is going well. Not only about the results, but also about how those results are achieved. Feedback is seen as support for learning (*#assessmentforlearning*), and giving and receiving feedback is a learning moment in itself (*#assessmentaslearning*).

Feedback does not always lead to better performance. In their meta-analysis including data from 12,652 individuals, Avraham Kluger and Angelo DeNisi[58] demonstrated that when individuals receive feedback about their performance, this leads to lower performance in one third of the studies. This means that in the majority of cases feedback does have a positive impact. But only from the mindset that feedback leads to learning and if you give it in an effective way. There are many rules about how you are supposed to give feedback that don't necessarily have that positive impact. You are supposed to address the issue from your perspective by starting sentences with I, and to pack negative things between positive things[59] *#sandwichtechnique*, et cetera. High Impact Team members adhere to four fundamental rules. Everything else is a natural consequence of those rules.

1. **The 'appreciation' rule:** you can apply every possible rule from every book you've read, but if you do not fundamentally respect the person you are talking to, he or she will notice and not accept your feedback. Period. You can be sharp and confrontational. But always keep in mind what you appreciate about the person you are talking to. If you really can't think of anything, then chances are very low that your feedback will be effective.

2. **The 'dare to be honest' rule:** too many people just don't have the guts to say what they really want to say. Or they beat around the bush to such an extent that those they address won't grasp their actual point.

3. **The 'positive intention' rule:** always give feedback with the intention of helping. If you give feedback only to vent your own frustrations, then you should not do it. Don't just say what people should do less often. Indicate what they can do more often: *feedforward*. If you give someone concrete support, there is a greater chance that he or she will actually do something with your feedback.

4. **The 'feedback on feedback' rule:** if feedback is misunderstood, if it undermines your relationship, or if it leaves a bad taste, then something went wrong. Try to see how your feedback landed and certainly ask for feedback on feedback if you have doubts about it.

In this chapter, I dissected and structured the concept of team learning as STEP at the team level and feedback at the team and individual level, but in reality it is a very chaotic and delicate process. STEP and feedback are constantly intertwined.[60] Internal and external feedback processes are crucial for each of the phases of the STEP model. For example, you will never be able to push the Stop button of your team without giving feedback. After all, pushing the Stop button in itself is already giving feedback. You indicate that something needs to be done. That you think the team can or should do better.

Feedback is also important in the Think and Evaluate phases. In an open feedback culture, team members can use each other as a sounding board during these phases. People ask for feedback and give their own opinion. People are asked about the reasons behind their opinions. They give positive feedback if they agree and criticize or give suggestions if they feel something is wrong with their colleagues' reasoning.

During the Proceed phase, feedback is essential because people rarely execute precisely what is decided in the team. That's normal. But without the habit of subsequently addressing each other about it, there is a good chance that the shared decision will not be executed. STEP requires team members who are able to and who dare to give, request and receive feedback.

PS: KIRSTEN'S TEAM

After the two-day seminar with Kirsten's team, many small STEP and feedback moments started to occur in and between meetings – thanks to their ability to learn. The offsite was just the starting point of a long process that turned the entire organization upside down, step by step. Many moments, late evenings, small interventions, et cetera during which something special happened time and time again. Before the offsite, the general vibe in the team, the organization, and the entire sector had been that growth was no longer possible. *Saturation* was the word you heard everywhere. A year after the offsite, the management team was 100 percent convinced that it was mainly their own mindset that had stopped them. Slowly but steadily something changed in the minds of almost all the team members. Afterwards, everything was different, both at the level of their ambition and at a more fundamental level: the way the team members saw themselves and each other. When I visited them again after a year, the mindset had changed radically: we are going to grow. The radical shift was not that the team had expressed a growth ambition. The radical shift was the fact that during those many STEP and feedback moments, team members had started to truly believe that growth was possible.

CHAPTER 3
SAFE TEAMING

The team had worked incredibly hard over the past four months. Launching a new software business with unique products does not happen without effort, and you never do it alone. Without feedback from the customers, the end users, and the team itself, the product would never have been what it is today: a software innovation that can triple the efficiency of digital production processes. Today, Lara – one of the product engineers – has the honor and pleasure of sending the first finished version to the first paying customer. She is nervous. The client is an early adopter with a huge network. If things go well with this customer, who knows what might happen. The sky is the limit. Only 20 minutes until the deadline. To be 100 percent sure that she is forwarding the correct version, Lara runs the program one last time. Only twelve percent speed gain? What? There's a bug in this version! A disaster. Speed is the added value for the customer. Somehow Lara had opened a beta version on the server and overwrote the finished version without noticing it.

Lara immediately realizes she has made a terrible mistake. This has never happened to her before. Her heart races, she feels her body temperature rising. Should she still send this version and act as if nothing happened? That would be a disaster for the team. Should she inform the team? Can't she solve it herself?

Situations like this happen to all of us, although the consequences are not always as severe as in the story of Lara. The physical response Lara experiences stems from a mix of emotions: anger, disappointment, doubt, and despair. But two emotions are always somewhere in the mix: fear and shame. *Fear*, because not only have I made a mistake, I will also have to come clean to my team about it at some point, and I will have to bear the consequences of my mistake. *Shame*, because I start to doubt my competence and because my first reaction was to figure out how I could make it look less bad.

Often, these emotions of fear and shame tend to trigger us to make things worse. There is only one context in which they are less of a barrier to reaching a solution: *safe teams*. In this chapter, I discuss the different building blocks of Safe Teaming and how you and your team can put them together.

WHAT IS DIFFERENT IN SAFE TEAMS?

People in safe teams are as imperfect as you and me. They make the same mistakes, have the same insecurities, fears, and reflexes. But there is one big difference: they dare to speak up when something feels wrong, because they trust that their colleagues and supervisor will not punish them for it. On the contrary, they believe they will get appreciation for doing so. Take the story of Lara as an example.

Within a few minutes after Lara had realized her mistake, she was already on the phone with Jerry, founder and CEO of the start-up. Lara tried to explain what had happened, but before she reached the end of her third sentence, she burst into tears. She felt so embarrassed. Convinced that she had destroyed the future of the young company.

Jerry kept calm. His first response was to listen, ask questions, dig deeper, until he understood exactly what had happened. Then, he reassured Lara. *'Heck, that really sucks, but you did the right thing by calling me.'* When Lara collected herself, she and Jerry made a plan to regain control of the situation. About fifteen minutes later, they both knew what they had to do. Jerry contacted the customer and explained the situation in full transparency. Lara contacted the team, explained what had happened and informed them about the action plan she and Jerry had created.

After an all-nighter with the entire team, the mistake was corrected. A few hours later, the product went live in the client organization. They had missed the deadline. Lara's mistake impacted the trust of her team and the client, and with reason. But the way they dealt with it as a team did so too. At the beginning of the next team meeting, something strange happened: the team leader thanked Lara for her courageous decision to share her mistake as soon as she did.

Each team encounters moments where things don't go as planned. If you are going through such moments in a team that is not safe, chances are higher that fear and shame will take over. If so, constructively changing the situation together becomes very hard. On the other hand, people in safe teams believe that it is safe to take interpersonal risks, speak openly and show vulnerability.

There are different kinds of interpersonal risk. What is considered to be an interpersonal risk depends on your team, the context in which you work, and your culture. But let's make one thing very clear. I am not talking about running down the hallway naked, breaking physical safety norms, inappropriately approaching colleagues, consistently ending your emails with insults to your CEO, or leaving doors, windows and closets open on purpose. Though these behaviors could also be considered as risky, they have nothing to do with opening up and being vulnerable. To be sure that we are on the same page, let me give you some specific examples of what kind of interpersonal risks I am talking about: asking questions when others think you should know the answer; openly disagreeing with someone of higher seniority; sharing personal stories about yourself, admitting you're struggling and asking for help; trying something out without being sure of the consequences; giving or asking for honest feedback.

PSYCHOLOGICAL SAFETY AT TEAM LEVEL

People in safe teams feel psychologically safe.[61] In the mid '90s, Amy Edmondson dusted off the long-established concept of psychological safety[62] on the individual level and translated it to the team level. This was prompted by her study of eight nursing teams in two different hospitals.[63] The study investigated possible predictors for mistakes in administering medication, discovering these mistakes and correcting them. Previous research showed that the margin of error can vary greatly between teams, even within the same hospital. On average, 2.3 to 23.7 errors per thousand patients were measured. Edmondson's most important question was this: which differences between teams can explain differences in that margin of error?

The design of her study was simple and elegant. One researcher registered the errors for each team. Then a second researcher – someone who knew nothing about the margins of error – conducted questionnaires, observed, and interviewed the teams. The results were unexpected. Edmondson expected that positive perceptions of teamwork, social relationships, and leadership would be associated with fewer errors, but the opposite was true: the more positive the perceptions about teamwork, team relationships, and team leadership, the more errors were registered.

Although counter-intuitive, these results can easily be explained. The teams differed on one crucial point: their assessment of the consequences of reporting errors. In teams with many reported errors, team members trusted that openness would be dealt with constructively. Teams with few reported errors feared punishment by the supervisor or colleagues. High Impact Teams with good relationships and coaching managers don't make more mistakes, they're just less afraid to report errors, discuss them openly and learn from them together.

Since the first empirical studies by Edmondson, the concept of team psychological safety has received increased attention. Today the concept is widely known. Google recently conducted a large-scale study on the effectiveness of their teams.[64] Over a two-year period, they studied 180 teams, looking at more than 250 variables. They concluded that *who* is on the team matters less than *how* the team members interact. Psychological safety was the first and by far the most important success factor in their teams. Other academic studies also describe psychological safety as a reliable predictor for good collaboration. A meta-analysis by Sanner and Bunderson investigated a total of 2,147 teams and showed a strong positive relationship between team psychological safety and team learning (58 percent) and between team psychological safety and team performance (32 percent).[65] And a recent meta-analysis (by Frazier et al. in 2017) with nearly 5,000 groups shows a positive relationship between psychological safety and task performance.[66] These strong positive relationships are robust. This means they exist in all kinds of settings – both in long-lasting teams and short-term projects, as Edmondson discussed in depth in her book *Teaming*.[67] And both within the boundaries of a collaboration and on the boundary between a collective and its environment as discussed in our penultimate chapter: Context.

In her 2008 article, *The Competitive Imperative of Learning*,[68] Edmondson clearly states that psychological safety has nothing to do with an 'anything goes' policy: *'Psychological safety is not about being nice – or about lowering performance standards. Quite the opposite: it's about recognizing that high performance requires the openness, flexibility, and interdependence that can develop only in a psychologically safe environment, especially when the situation is changing or complex. Psychological safety makes it possible to give tough feedback and have difficult conversations – which demand trust and respect – without the need to tiptoe around the truth.'* She explains how some managers find it difficult to grasp the benefits of psychological safety because they assume that psychological safety and keeping each other accountable are total opposites. She illustrates how psychological safety and accountability go together perfectly in organizations that perform well. They even reinforce each other. When it's unclear what you will be held accountable for, you will feel less safe to act. Why? Because the boundaries within which you can behave are unclear, even nonexistent. One false move, and it could cost you your head. By clearly defining the boundaries of the playing field, people will feel safer to take the interpersonal risks required to perform on a higher level.

PSYCHOLOGICAL
SAFETY HIGH

COMFORT
ZONE

LEARNING
ZONE

ACCOUNTABILITY
LOW

ACCOUNTABILITY
HIGH

APATHY
ZONE

ANXIETY
ZONE

PSYCHOLOGICAL
SAFETY LOW

ASSERTIVENESS VERSUS SAFETY

Team psychological safety is often falsely confused with the assertiveness of individual team members. I vividly remember a CEO of a bank illustrating this in a meeting with his extended management team. Some team members were courageous enough to admit that they didn't feel safe enough to give him feedback. They also explicitly explained how his attitude towards feedback contributed to this feeling. His reaction? *'Bullshit. Whether you have the guts to speak up doesn't depend on me or your colleagues. It depends entirely on you. I expect people working at this level to be assertive enough to open their mouths. Big cars, big wages, big hairy balls. End of story.'* You gotta love the irony.

This manager equates psychological safety with the assertiveness of his team members, but in reality there is a big difference between the two. Assertiveness is a personality trait or a competence of individual team members. Team psychological safety is a dynamic characteristic of the team as a whole.

In addition, team members – regardless of how assertive they are – make relatively similar assessments of how psychologically safe their team is.[69] Therefore, team psychological safety is not just about how assertive the individual team members are to break through the existing social barriers in the team. It is also about the shared assessment of how high or low those social barriers are in the team. In a psychologically safe team, the social barriers are lower, so it requires less energy, assertiveness or courage to jump over them and to engage in socially risky behavior.

By the way, the manager from the example above is wrong on two counts. Research on psychological safety in teams shows that the behavior of the supervisor does play a crucial role.[70] That is one reason why psychological safety so often differs between teams within the same organization.

The fact that psychological safety has a robust positive effect on team learning and performance does not make it easy to build safe teams. Why is Safe Teaming so difficult?

To answer that question, I want to take you back to the time of *Homo erectus*. 1.8 million years ago, a man's working day consisted largely of hunting and gathering. Based on historical research, anthropologists Gurven and Kaplan estimate that only 57 percent of hunter-gatherers reached the age of fifteen, with an average life expectancy of somewhere between 21 and 37.[71] It should be clear that in those days people were confronted with physically dangerous situations almost every working day. And I'm not talking about 'if I replace the staples in my stapler, I could hurt my fingers' situations. I am talking about *life-or-death* situations: attacks by wild animals or members of another tribe.

Back then, our brain was already equipped with two amygdalae[72] – two small almond-shaped spheres that are hidden somewhere in the temporal lobe of our brain. They are part of the limbic system responsible for processing emotions and they help us in recognizing life-threatening situations and responding to them immediately. They are our so-called survival instinct. Today, they still work in exactly the same way. The moment we see a bear in the distance, the *danger*-alarm in our amygdalae is activated and a fight-or-flight mode is automatically triggered: '*Act first, think later.*'[73] Depending on the situation, we will either fight or run like hell.

In the era of the *Homo erectus*, this reflex was essential for survival. Homo erecti with poorly developed amygdalae didn't stand a chance. *Survival of the fittest* ensured that our amygdalae kept on developing. But the amygdalae do a poor job in distinguishing between physically and emotionally risky situations. Our internal alarms go off in both cases. As a result, they now trigger us repeatedly in the hunting areas of our contemporary work life: meeting rooms. At work, we regularly face situations in which we risk being seen as incompetent, ignorant, negative, meddlesome, insecure, and so on. They trigger our amygdalae and the fear of losing face or being excluded. Admitting a mistake? No way! I don't want others to think I am incompetent; I'd rather tell a little lie. Asking questions? No way! I don't want them to see me as intrusive, meddling or ignorant. Challenge colleagues or give critical feedback? No way! They will see me as negative, arrogant or a know-it-all!

Being open to critical feedback? No way! Not without first fighting to prove I'm right and someone else is wrong. Asking for help or feedback? No way! That could be seen as weak or insecure.[74]

Our amygdalae tend to make it difficult for us to speak openly and show vulnerability. They ensure just the opposite: that we protect ourselves in order to not get hurt. But vulnerability is, unfortunately, exactly what each of those social risks demand. Brené Brown defines vulnerability as defying uncertainties, taking risks and exposing yourself emotionally.[75] In a way, doing so is always socially risky. Showing who you really are, what you really want, what you really feel or what you really think. That means you can really get hurt.

NOBODY SAID IT WAS EASY

It can be complex to build psychological safety because numerous variables affect it. For example, team psychological safety tends to relate negatively to group size.[76] The larger the group, the more difficult it is for people to be open and vulnerable. That's why I often divide teams into smaller groups when I want them to have deeper or more vulnerable discussions. Internal competition or negative interdependence[77] are also related to lower levels of psychological safety. The same goes for a hierarchical organization in which power and status prevail.[78]

I'd like to highlight one last reason why it is so difficult to build psychological safety: you cannot *fake* it. You cannot create a sense of psychological safety without actually making it safer. Team members will never feel safe if their supervisor is a bully who promotes a culture of *shaming and blaming*. Therefore, the ultimate test for psychological safety is the actual response to socially risky behavior. If you show social daring and there is no constructive response, if you are punished in any way for doing so, then psychological safety will decrease. Not only did you burn yourself, your colleagues have witnessed what happened.

In other words, building psychological safety is not just about preventing your own fight-or-flight reaction, it is also about how others respond to social daring. To build a safe team, everyone in the team must learn how to react to someone showing social daring: instead of jumping into fight-or-flight mode and getting overwhelmed by negative emotions, we need to *learn* to move into a broaden-and-build mode and thrive on positive emotions. Barbara Fredrickson called it a broaden-and-build mode, because positive emotions broaden your repertoire of thoughts and actions, and build up your personal resources.[79] With a broaden-and-build mode, your vision and your actions will not narrow, as in the fight-or-flight mode. On the contrary, you will deal with the situation with more overview, more creativity, more consideration, more openness and more efficiency. You will join forces and discuss how you can best deal with the difficult situation together.[80]

It takes time and energy to build a psychologically safe team and to learn how to respond consistently from a broaden-and-build mode. Unfortunately, one well-placed fight-or-flight response can be enough to break down the slowly built safety. *'See, he can't be trusted. Told you so.'* Team psychological safety is hard to build, but very easy to break. The greatest challenge 21st century teams are facing is to make better use of their physically safe environment by turning it into a psychologically safe environment.

DIFFICULT, BUT NOT IMPOSSIBLE!

Don't worry: it is possible to build a safe team, even if it has gone drastically wrong in the past. Psychological safety is perception and perception is reality. But perceptions are never carved in stone. Psychological safety is constantly moving, and everyone in and around the team can influence it. It does not matter whether you are an external coach, a manager, or one of the team members. Below you will find five insights into how you can influence the psychological safety in your team:

1. **Frame:** create a clear framework with clear agreements. Make explicit which socially risky behaviors you expect from each other. What are not just *nice-to-haves*, but *must-haves*?

2. **Be brave:** set the example yourself. Setting the framework, people rationally *know* what risky behavior is expected, but they only start to *believe* it emotionally when they see you doing it. Especially if you are the manager.

3. **Reward:** reward people who take social risks and show vulnerability. Ask them questions, listen and respond constructively. Start with a positive focus on the people who *do* support psychological safety.

4. **Coach:** the switch to a safe team is not easy for some people. Coach by listening, questioning, understanding, but also by keeping people accountable when they don't stick to the behavioral agreements. First give feedback on behavior, before turning to feedback on results.

5. **Follow through:** if coaching someone extensively does not work, if someone keeps killing the psychological safety in the team time after time after time, then consequences are required. If there are no consequences, you send a signal to the entire team that you are not really serious about the agreements made. In some cases, dismissal or a transfer to another team may even be necessary.

I deliberately talk about five insights and not five steps. Why? The road may seem logical and many teams follow a similar path, but in reality everything is intertwined. Nevertheless, there is one thing you can always count on: it will be an exciting, fragile and emotionally charged process every time. Because people tend to find it uncomfortable to talk about vulnerability and psychological safety. Because working on psychological safety paradoxically tends to require social courage. And because there isn't a single process that offers you 100 percent guarantee of success.

1. FRAME: YOU CAN LEARN SAFE TEAMING TOGETHER AND IT STARTS WITH A CLEAR FRAMEWORK – AGREEMENTS ABOUT HOW YOU WILL WORK TOGETHER AND WHAT BEHAVIOR YOU EXPECT FROM EACH OTHER.

People sometimes feel unsafe because they are in an unknown situation. You could compare the situation to that of a three-year-old girl who is dropped off at a new daycare center for the very first time, without much preparation or explanation from her parents. Imagine being that girl. You learned to talk a few months ago and you recently managed to go to the toilet by yourself. You are scared. You are dropped into a situation that is completely unknown to you. What could your caregivers do to increase psychological safety? The way they treat you matters a great deal, but they can also help you by creating a safety framework. A first corner of that framework concerns the purpose, the why of your visit to daycare

(Visioning). They immediately make it a lot safer if they can explain why mom and dad left you there, when they will pick you up again, and that you are supposed to play a lot and have fun in the meantime. A second corner of the framework concerns the organization of the daycare centre (Organizing). It incorporates the structure of the day; the structure of the building; where you can hang your coat; where the toilet is – and that you can decide to go there without asking, et cetera. A third corner concerns the other individuals in the daycare center, the other children and the caregivers. An important way to increase psychological safety is by immediately taking some time to get to know each other and doing something fun together. They can help you to make some new friends (Individual Impact).

In fact, it is the same in teams, but we often pretend that we are old and wise enough to function without a safety framework. Sometimes new colleagues take years to discover and understand the vision, organization and individual manuals of their colleagues. *'In this team, you have to earn appreciation.'* How much safer would it feel if colleagues were given a framework and appreciation from the start? Know that the way new employees are welcomed to your team is a mirror of your team's culture. A fourth and final corner of the safety framework concerns the behavioral rules in the daycare centre. To put it simply: the do's and don'ts. I elaborate on this last corner below.

But first I'd like to take you from that daycare center in Europe to one of the largest slums on this planet: Kibera in Nairobi, Kenya. I'm walking through the narrow thoroughfares between the corrugated iron houses. Because I have been on the road for a long time, I pause to stretch at a small opening in the jungle of slums. A dozen children are playing soccer with a homemade rag ball. They come from different neighborhoods in Kibera to meet at this small square. They play wild and fierce like real professionals in a World Cup final. I notice that there is no referee. They tackle, make mistakes and apologize, let the other team take penalties and so on. Right before I leave, I ask one of the older boys how it works. *'How do you manage to combine playing so hard with having so much fun without needing a referee?'* He grins from ear to ear. *'No referee? We are all referees!'* The boy explains to me how the different neighborhoods play according to different rules. But just before they start playing, they agree on a number of things. Do we play with offside or not? Is there a goalkeeper or not? Is tackling allowed or not? And from then on everyone is a referee.

The fourth corner of the safety framework concerns the rules of conduct. Far too often we assume that it is clear what the *right* behavior is and that people will dare to act accordingly. That people will dare to play hard and fair. Most of the time it is not clear and often people are afraid of behaving according to what is actually right. Why? Not only because we have different backgrounds and play according to different rules. But also because we are all, to a certain extent, intuitively afraid that the positive image others hold of us will be damaged. If you want your people to feel safe enough to display the *right* socially risky behavior, it is crucial to make the rules of the game clear.

Very often, teams have clear frameworks and rules. The *what needs to be done* is often very explicit. Some organizations have rock-solid operating systems with hundreds of Key Performance Indicators. Our organizations are saturated with these *hard frames*. But when it comes to behavior or *how we should act*, such frameworks are often lacking. The motto is simple: *'Just act normal!'* But what is normal? A lot of teams miss a behavioral framework or *soft frame* to turn their physically safe environment into an environment that is also psychologically safe.

The specific agreements for an effective *soft frame* can only be determined by the team itself. Usually a soft frame is about very simple things. Things others expect from you. Things you expect from them. But most importantly, things we all find difficult to do. Like giving feedback immediately if something goes wrong; if you give me feedback, do it like this; do not interrupt others; no laptops or other mobile devices during the meeting, et cetera. *'Seriously? It sounds like you think we're still in kindergarten.'* I hear you. But creating a soft frame is not about restating the obvious. It's not about creating lists of behavioral rules and regulations that you all find obvious. Then what is it about? Many *soft frames* are quite similar, but they are only powerful if they take into account three principles:

- **Principle 1: make sure it fits your unique identity.** The more closely the framework fits the team, the more powerful it will be. Be original, use your own words and make sure it is connected to *who* you are. Don't include any agreements that are already normal or obvious to you. Choose those things that are most likely to go wrong.

- **Principle 2: do not exaggerate the number of agreements.** I usually try to obey Miller's Law: *'The magic number is seven, plus or minus two.'*[81] *'Simple, clear purpose and principles give rise to complex and intelligent behavior. Complex rules and regulations give rise to simple and stupid behavior'.*[82] If people cannot easily remember the soft frame, it completely loses its power.

- **Principle 3: set agreements about how you want to keep the soft frame alive.** Always include an agreement that you immediately give each other open and honest feedback when you feel that someone is not following the defined soft frame. A soft frame only becomes a reality when team members confront each other when someone is not sticking to the agreements they have established.

But how do you reach those agreements? It all depends on what kind of collaboration we are talking about and also on what kind of position you hold. If you are collaborating with people for just one hour, it doesn't make sense to organize a workshop of 45 minutes to discuss the behavioral rules of the game. But maybe it is worthwhile to create a micro soft frame, for example, by stating clearly that you expect people to speak up if something is bothering them and by asking if it is all right if you do the same. If you are a team member in a team with a hierarchical leader, then you might not have the mandate to facilitate a discussion with your team to co-create a soft frame. You might start off by building your personal soft frame in one to ones with your peers and your manager, clarifying mutual expectations. If that works out well, you might be able to clarify and convince your team leader why it would be great to co-create a soft frame at the team level. In any case, you'll be more successful if you can clarify what you want (feedforward) and why, compared to complaining about what you miss. And sometimes just asking if you may facilitate a short workshop on rules of the game is sufficient to get the mandate for doing so.

Reflect together on how safe the team is and what your team's weak points are: look for specific situations in which you already feel safe and situations in which you do not yet feel safe. Furthermore, discuss specific situations when things did or did not work out. Talk to each other about these situations, give them meaning, try to analyze why something worked or not. Use metaphors, drawings, Post-its, whatever works for you. And come to explicit agreements that all of you believe will help. Whatever agreements or actions you come up with, you will still need to jump into the deep together to test whether they actually help you to collaborate more effectively. Every soft frame is imperfect. If you do not continue to adjust and refine it, it becomes redundant at some point. Don't be afraid to get rid of frameworks or to delete rules that have become habits. Dead frames are heavy and cost energy and money. Living frames – or frameworks that support you in the here and now to do what the customers and the team need from you – are light and generate energy. The essence is not the framework itself, but the behavior and habits that are supported by the framework.[83]

2. BE BRAVE: EVERYTHING DEPENDS ON YOUR COURAGE TO TAKE SOCIAL RISKS AND SET THE EXAMPLE YOURSELF!

Imagine the following situation: you have been working for a year at a company where hierarchy is important. Your manager unexpectedly asks you to participate in an important meeting; he wants you to be there because of your specific, valuable expertise. In the meeting room: your boss, the colleague with the longest track record, the CEO of the company and your biggest customer. You see a contract lying in the middle of the table.

The discussion runs its course, and suddenly you notice that there is a shift in the atmosphere. The customer starts to smile. Your CEO as well. Your boss and your colleague follow. It is obvious. They have seen the light. Together they will move in the direction of X in the coming years. You think: X? X is the totally wrong direction! You are not sure. You don't know which direction it should be, but you feel that everyone will get into trouble if you move towards X. This is the largest contract in the history of the company. It's now five seconds before the contract is signed. What do you do?

To be honest, I don't have a solution for this problem. There isn't one right answer. What I do know is that this situation requires you to take a social risk. What I also know is that the chances are very small that you made – or will ever make – a soft frame for such a specific situation. My advice? Do not tune out. Use the adrenaline that rises to keep an open mind. Look at the opportunities that present themselves in this crisis instead of the roadblocks. Broaden-and-build. And do something. Do it with an open mind and do what your conscience tells you to do. Do not hide behind the fact that you cannot know for sure what the consequences will be.

There are two good reasons why it pays off to take social risks, even in situations where it is not entirely clear what the consequences will be. First, it's about your life. Do you act the way you think you should act in good conscience? By default, those socially risky situations require a quick (re)action. They happen here and now, and if you don't respond now, the moment will be gone forever. You may feel guilty, imagine scenarios of how you could have acted differently and wonder what the result would have been. Nothing is more satisfying than acting in line with your own values and norms.

Secondly, the main way you build up psychological safety is by showing social daring. Some researchers seem to assume that there is a kind of linear causality between soft framing, psychological safety and social daring and that it runs in one direction: soft framing creates psychological safety in the team, which increases social daring. That seems logical. But it's wrong. People who work in teams know that it's wrong. Team members don't look at the soft frame on the wall to consider whether or not it is psychologically safe. They look at what others are doing. If you want to build a safe team, there is *always* one crucial anchor point, and that is your behavior. Make yourself vulnerable. Do it. Others will see it and that will help to lower the barrier for them to do the same.

If you have a position of power in the team, it is crucial to be aware of the shadow that you cast. Research shows that people with lower status in the group generally feel less psychologically safe than people with higher status.[84] It's not that easy to change. Establishing a soft frame helps team members to *know* which behavior is safe and which behavior is not. But people will only *feel* it in their stomachs or in their hearts when they see that their manager exemplifies it. And that is precisely what many managers forget to do. Almost all managers think it's okay for their team members to show vulnerability by admitting mistakes and apologizing for them, asking questions when they don't understand something, asking for feedback, and so on. But many forget to model it themselves. A good behavioral framework ensures that people realize what behavior is expected and why. It sows the seeds for psychological safety. But setting the example yourself ensures that people actually start to believe it. That's what makes the seeds grow.

Before I go to the next insight, I want to go back to that meeting with your colleague, your boss, the CEO and the client. I want to add one thing: be brave, but don't be stupid. It is *brave* to dare to do what you believe is right in an unpredictable situation that requires immediate action. But it is totally *stupid* to try to be brave in a situation that will definitely go wrong. Imagine for a moment that the contract will not be signed within five seconds, but only within an hour. You might consider stopping to check whether you are wearing a parachute before you jump from the plane. Ask yourself at least four questions:

- Are the **intentions** of the others towards you positive? Or are you in a competitive situation where others actually want you to lose? Is it possible to test the temperature of the water before jumping in?
- Do the people around the table behave with **integrity**? How do they interact with other people? How have they reacted in similar circumstances? What is their track record in that regard?
- Are there **agreements** about how you treat each other and is what you plan to do in line with that? If there are no agreements, is it possible to make agreements before jumping? First, announce how you want to give feedback and why. Again, jumping with a parachute is always safer than without.
- **How do others see you?** Do they trust your intentions, integrity and competence? What about your track record? Will you be able to convince them and reassure them that your intentions are pure? Can they trust you?

Apply this golden rule: '*Never ASS-U-ME, it makes an ASS out of U and ME.*'[85] And that goes both ways: do not blindly assume that it is possible, but neither assume that it is not.

3. REWARD: REWARD OTHERS WHEN THEY TAKE SOCIAL RISKS AND SHOW VULNERABILITY BY ASKING, LISTENING AND RESPONDING CONSTRUCTIVELY.

If you really want to create a *safe space* within which your team can function at a higher level, it is important to explicitly reward those who show vulnerability. You can do this in different ways. Take the example of how Jerry responded to Lara's mistake at the start of this chapter. When did he reward her for admitting the mistake?

One clear moment was of course when Jerry thanked Lara for her courage in the next team meeting. Lara didn't feel as if she had acted bravely at all. On the contrary, she felt she had made a fool of herself. She felt really uncomfortable that Jerry reminded her of her mistake by thanking her in front of the whole team. As if he wanted to rub it in again. But Jerry knew what he was doing and why he was doing it. Everyone knew that the mistake Lara made had harmed the team. Reminding the team was definitely not the reason Jerry mentioned it again. He had two other reasons. On the one hand, he wanted to make clear that he appreciates and expects everyone in the team to show vulnerability, even when serious mistakes are made. On the other hand, he had sensed that Lara was still upset. By putting it back on the table, he gave Lara and the team the opportunity to address the elephant in the room, to smooth things out and to learn some lessons from this experience. Later Lara acknowledged how that team meeting helped her to relieve her burden of guilt and start over.

But in addition to that team meeting, there was another, much more important moment where Jerry rewarded Lara for showing vulnerability. The moment he answered the phone. He asked questions and listened instead of tensing up. He didn't judge. He focused on learning by constructively looking for solutions with Lara. In that moment, Jerry built psychological safety by suppressing his own *fight-or-flight* reflex and responding from a *broaden-and-build* mode. Ultimately, that's the greatest reward for social daring. That is what makes people feel safe to do it again later on.

Unfortunately, staying *broaden-and-build* in such situations is a huge challenge. Often the social daring of one team member – giving feedback, admitting a mistake and so on – is an emotional threat to others. This explains why it is so difficult to respond constructively in those critical moments. You don't only have to recognize the social daring of the other person, but also recognize your own *fight-or-flight* mode in time.

When my *fight-or-flight* mode is activated, I feel a kind of tension between my heart and my head. It's my body warning me that I feel attacked or unsafe. That feeling might be different for you. But one thing's for sure: if you do not recognize your own *fight-or-flight* response in time, there is little to no chance that you will respond constructively. You'll run away or you'll counter attack, which will trigger negative consequences. Your colleagues will turn their backs, your *fight-or-flight* mode will kick in and safety will drop. Do you know what your *fight-or-flight* mode feels like? No? Try visualizing it. You will find that the next time it comes up, you will be much more aware of what is happening and how you can deal with it.

The way I describe rewarding social daring makes it seem simple. Someone shows socially risky behavior as agreed on in the soft frame, you recognize it, thank the person by listening, and respond constructively. And you make it clear to the team that you expect such behavior. But it's not that easy. Why? Because social daring sometimes arrives in disguise. If you're not paying attention, you won't even notice it.

Social daring does not happen only during the big critical moments. It also shows in hundreds or even thousands of mini-moments. Moments when team members subtly indicate – without a large neon-lit *this was a mistake* sign – that something has gone wrong. They implicitly or very carefully ask for understanding or attention. They give indirect feedback. Sometimes they don't even say anything at all and hope that someone will read it on their faces. From your perspective, they have taken a social mini-risk, but for them it really meant something.

Even in those little moments, it is important that you reward by picking up the signal and using it to learn together. Even in those little moments, a negative or uninterested reaction, or the absence of any reaction negatively influences psychological safety in the team. During my doctoral research, I did hundreds of observation sessions in teams.[86] Sometimes there were team members who shared a crazy idea, made a critical remark, or something similar. They took a social risk that the others in the team could have seized as an opportunity to learn as a team. But often no one reacted at all. In one meeting, I vividly remember a team member risking her neck five times by making a provocative suggestion. I am sure the team would have solved the problem if at least one team member had listened to her suggestions and asked her questions, if at least one had reacted constructively. But even more importantly, interviews after the team had completed the project clearly showed that the lack of a reaction in that meeting was not only *caused* by a lack of psychological safety, it also *negatively influenced* psychological safety.

Of course we sometimes react the wrong way. Shit happens. When it happens, you can be sure that it will affect psychological safety. However, you can counter the negative effect by explicitly apologizing, admitting your mistake, and asking what you can do to make it right. This works well once or twice. But the more you have to apologize, the less your excuses will be worth. Prevention is better than cure.

The conclusion is simple: when someone in your team has the courage to show vulnerability, be sure to respond in a way that makes it worth the risk. Team psychological safety is created by the courage to speak, but equally by the empathetic response that follows. A reaction that causes something constructive to happen. A response that shows that people remain worthwhile, even when they have made a mistake.

4. COACH: EVERYONE REFEREE, EVERYONE COACH.

For some people, the switch to a culture of appreciation of social risk-taking and mutual accountability is not obvious. Don't assume that it is sufficient to agree on a behavioral framework, set a good example, and reward the early adopters from the start. Many people were rewarded for years to come up with solutions and show how well they were doing, rather than to ask questions and show vulnerability. It is naive to expect that everyone will start showing vulnerability just because it has been agreed upon and others are setting the example.

That is why it is important not only to reward people who show the right behavior from the start, but also to coach people who find it difficult to do so. There will be times when people fail to honor the rules of engagement. Imagine that someone in your team doesn't dare to flag a certain problem or give feedback. But you do not notice it and do not respond to it. After a while, the standards and the psychological safety will start to fade. Your soft frame and your exemplary behavior become meaningless. Safe teams are safe because everyone is a referee and everyone is a coach.

Let's go back to Jerry's team for a moment. Imagine the scenario in which Lara did not share her discovery with Jerry. Imagine she chose to pretend nothing had happened and just sent the slower test version to the customer. That the customer, who expected much faster performance, reacted furiously. A big blow to the team. No one understood what had happened or why. But Matthew, one of Lara's colleagues, decided to run the test version again and discovered that Lara had concealed the error. Imagine how it shocked him. The whole team had agreed to the *no cover-up*-policy. Together they had made the promise that errors should always be admitted immediately, so that necessary steps could be taken to find solutions. And as far as he could remember, Lara was there when they decided to implement this policy!

How would you react if you were Matthew? Be aware that your reaction matters, but that things can go wrong on a number of points:

- Risk 1: you immediately focus on the *what*. When you address Lara about the error you discovered, there is a risk that the conversation will be about the error itself: '*What is the error? What is the solution?*' Though very important, these questions are secondary. In safe teams, people first and foremost focus on the *how*. '*How come you didn't discuss this error with someone as soon as you could?*'

- Risk 2: you get angry, you forget to ask questions and you forget to listen. If Lara finds it difficult to admit her mistake, that may mean that something is blocking her. Breaking a rule of conduct is often a symptom of an underlying problem. The real risk is that by getting angry you focus overly on the symptom and lose sight of the disease.

- Risk 3: you perfectly understand what has happened, but you don't give feedback. You don't talk to Lara about it '*Because that's not my job, right? What would she think of me? Giving feedback is the manager's job, isn't it?*' Perhaps you do have the courage to discuss it with other colleagues at the coffee machine. Behind Lara's back. In safe teams, everyone gives feedback to everyone and they do it now, right away. Especially when it is about the *how*. Just like the football players in Kibera who were all acting as referees. Referees whistle during the match, not after the match.

The best thing you can do for Lara and the entire team is to help Lara admit her mistake to the team and then look for ways to act differently in future. That is what I mean by *coaching*. Again, there is no general formula for effective coaching, except perhaps this one: first understand, then try to be understood.[87] In Chapter 6 – Individual Impact – I elaborate on what it means for team members to act as a coach. But for now, I just want to talk about one common reason why we don't like to address our mistakes and those of others.

We often experience failure immediately as fault. Edmondson writes that this problem is one of the main reasons that we are failing to build psychologically safe teams: *'Failure and fault are virtually inseparable in most households, organizations, and cultures. Every child learns at some point that admitting failure means taking the blame. That is why so few organizations have shifted to a culture of psychological safety in which the rewards of learning from failure can be fully realized.'*[88] We tend to apportion guilt for almost every failure. Preferably, to somebody else. And boom, psychological safety flies out of the window. It is easy to blame someone for a mistake. But the real question is whether it is always necessary. In some situations, it makes sense to blame someone. If Lara made the same mistake time and time again out of carelessness, if she refused Matthew's helping hand, or if she was making a mistake deliberately, then it could make sense to blame her. But is that the case? No. Research shows that team leaders and managers in organizations report they can identify a legitimate offender in only three to five percent of the mistakes that happen. These same team leaders and managers also report that of all errors – for which they think that no one should be *blamed* – 70 to 90 percent are treated as if someone is *to blame*.[89] Think about errors like accidents, system errors, errors from experiments, and so on. The consequence of mixing up failure and guilt makes people less likely to admit mistakes and respond defensively when they receive feedback.[90]

5. FOLLOW THROUGH: IF SOMEONE IS REALLY NOT ABLE OR WILLING TO PARTICIPATE IN SAFE TEAMING – EVEN AFTER A LONG PERIOD OF FEEDBACK AND COACHING – CONSEQUENCES MUST FOLLOW.

Roger has been working for the team for years. He knows his job inside out. He is *Mister Perfect*. But Roger explodes when things go wrong. He starts ranting and raving. He loves gossiping about his colleagues who seem to fail time and time again. Recently Roger got a new manager: Simon. Simon is different. He wants to build a safe team. But Roger does not want to participate in that soft feedback nonsense. He doesn't believe in it. His entire career was built on delivering perfect results. Backbiting, expertise and intimidation were his three main ingredients for career progression. So Roger knows the art of keeping the gossip mill going. Simon discovered Roger's habit of gossiping and started to understand how he had a negative influence on the psychological safety of the team. He made a number of clear agreements with the team and with Roger. But Roger kept refusing to adhere to them. Every time Simon set the example by being vulnerable, Roger tried to abuse it. Simon systematically gave Roger feedback when he crossed the line and thanked him every time he did well, even though that seldom happened. It all slid smoothly off Roger's elephant skin. Sometimes Roger feigned a cooperative maneuver, giving Simon the feeling he could still have an impact on him. But basically nothing ever changed.

What do you do in such a case? Someone like Roger needs your coaching. But what if his toxic behavior continues? Then you unwillingly start the dismissal procedure with a negative evaluation. If you were to give up at a certain point and let Roger continue his behavior, you will not only disappoint yourself, you will disappoint all those who started to hope for a workplace where they would no longer waste energy on *fear* and *shame*. In essence, you give the signal that you are not at all serious about Safe Teaming.

In practice, I notice that people who have not adjusted their behavior after many efforts sometimes suddenly make a U-turn when you start to show that you mean it. For example, by proposing a change of team, denying a bonus or starting a dismissal procedure. It seems some people only realize that you are serious about the agreements made if you react in a serious way when they don't adhere to them. It may sound a little crazy – increasing psychological safety by starting a dismissal procedure. But we sometimes underestimate the devastating effect of endlessly postponing consequences.

PS: There are situations in which it is not feasible to start the firing procedure, for example, because you live in a country with a legal barrier or because the person involved is someone with a unique talent. But then you have to resort to damage control very explicitly; so explicitly that both the team and the person know that it is an exception, the way you will deal with this exception and why. If they cannot live with that, they will leave. So be it. I remember a software team that kept a first class bully on board. He was one of only three people on this planet who was able to crack certain security codes. And he knew it. Do know that you are playing with fire by keeping him. What do you do with the next exception and the next, and then yet another? You cannot build psychological safety without actually making it safe.

Safe Teaming is a crucial corner of the HIT model. Without psychological safety, there is little chance that team members will commit themselves openly and honestly. On the contrary, there is a good chance that they will pretend. Team learning, Visioning and Organizing turn into a mirage without truth and without impact. Safe Teaming is crucial for High Impact Teaming, because authentic interactions form the basis for surfacing the real talents, concerns, ideas and ambitions. It is the basis to really learn, to really lift your team to a higher level and ultimately to really win. This chapter aimed on the one hand to make that point, and on the other, to explain how High Impact Teams engage in Safe Teaming.

However, there is another reason why Safe Teaming matters, regardless of winning or losing. Safe Teaming creates space for a deeper form of connection: connection based on authenticity.

How does Safe Teaming relate to being connected on the basis of authenticity? Well, Safe Teaming helps you and your colleagues to be vulnerable in your interaction with one another.[91] In her research, Brené Brown finds that that is exactly what is needed to create authentic connections. People are imperfect. Therefore, the only authentic attitude is an attitude that also shows the flaws. You cannot really show the way you are without showing your dark and more sensitive sides. But if you show *the real you*, you run the risk of *really* getting hurt. That is the price you pay for stepping out of your armor.

> *Authenticity is a collection of choices that we have to make every day. It's about the choice to show up and be real. The choice to be honest. The choice to let our true selves be seen.*
> – BRENÉ BROWN[92]

Safe Teaming makes it safer to be vulnerable. As such, it promotes the choice to be authentic and to develop authentic connections. But I can immediately hear some skeptics contend that the prize isn't worth the effort. People who might have had bad experiences with showing vulnerability. Who learned along the way that life is a poker game that you lose when you let others look at your cards. That psychological safety is a myth, connectedness, a naive dream and authenticity, therefore, a stupid choice. A choice that does not belong in a professional environment. A choice that renders no guarantee for success whatsoever.

Those skeptics – just like a large part of the world's population – go to work every day wearing a mask. They do so because they feel that they should always be on their guard and keep their distance; that who they really are is insufficient or doesn't matter; and that their real feelings, desires and talents do not belong in a professional environment.

There is some truth to their line of thought. Authenticity offers no guarantee whatsoever of authentic connectedness and success. But even skeptics must recognize that not showing vulnerability has a price as well; that those who hide in armor not only avoid or flatten the negative emotions such as shame, disappointment, and sadness, but also the positive ones – passion, friendship, joy, pride, desire, trust, et cetera. All those are impossible without vulnerability. Isn't it a pity to deny ourselves the things that really matter? Safe Teaming can help us to deal with practical problems – such as finding an error in a software package 20 minutes before it has to go to the customer – in a more constructive way. But much more than that, it is a gateway to authentic connection and experiencing things that really matter. According to Brown, that's the meaning of life. [93]

You will never hear me say that it will all be puppies and champagne. Because when authentic connection and therefore vulnerability become the norm, it won't only be the successes and connections that start to feel more intense. The fights will also be fiercer and the punches will hit you harder. Everything will become more personal. But in the heat of battle, you will feel that you are alive. And when the dust starts to settle, there won't just be impact. There will be a strong connection that feels warm, and that lasts forever.

CHAPTER 4

VISIONING

Munich 1972, the Olympic kayaking finale, category K-4, 1 kilometer. Nine boats at the start. Ready to go. Four well-trained bodies in each boat. If you zoom in on the first boat, you see four men with their paddles ready. The athlete sitting in the front seat has his mind set on one thing and one thing only: gold. Winning silver means losing gold. He has trained for eight years of his life to succeed in this very moment. He would rather die after 500 meters than not give everything he's got. The second athlete in the boat. He is overwhelmed by the audience and the cameras. In his mind he is waving to his parents. *'Hi Mommy, hi Daddy, I'm in the finals!'* Being in the final in itself exceeds his wildest expectations and now he's just going to enjoy the ride. Pierre de Coubertin: *'Participating is better than winning.'*[94] The third athlete in the boat. *'Let this moment last forever. Away from the problems at home, the divorce, the sale of the house...'* For the fourth and final athlete, the story is simple. He just can't wait to start: *'Sport, let's move! It's the best placebo for my Ritalin. GO!'* Four people in the boat at the highest level. What are the chances that this boat will win the final of the K4?[95]

None. At this level, the physical capacities of the participants in each boat are more or less the same. So what makes the difference? Visioning. If you appear at the start without an aligned vision, you won't stand a chance. All four athletes must be aligned on how they sit in the boat and on the ambition of the team. But you don't align on essentials like that ten seconds before the race. This is something you started doing on the first training camp eight years ago. And then you do it again and again and again. Take it from someone who has experience with races at that level. Someone I admire: former Olympic kayaking finalist, and founder of Unicorn, Paul Stinckens.

Top teams distinguish themselves by Visioning.[96] Visioning is the process through which you co-create a shared picture of where you stand, where you want to go and how you want to bridge the gap between the two. When the shared vision reflects the essence and the truth for each of the team members, it will not only give the team direction, but also a huge dose of energy, an overview, focus and courage. Creating a shared vision is not about forcing everyone to sit in the boat in exactly the same way. Having different individual ambitions is okay. But teams are aware of the way everybody is sitting in the boat, and they succeed in bringing their ambitions together – to reinforce one another. Like a laser cannon that combines slightly different light sources into one powerful beam. It is not about agreeing 100 percent on every point. What matters is that you agree on the key points, and you harvest the power of diversity on everything else. And it isn't just classical teams that work together for years who thrive on Visioning; even if you have a meeting with people you have never met before and you will never meet again, clarifying the purpose of the meeting at the start will make you 100% more effective.

If everyone is thinking alike, then somebody isn't thinking.

– GEORGE PATTON[97]

Recently I visited some friends for coffee – Peter, Sophie and their seven-year-old daughter, Martha. At a certain point, Sophie told Martha that I was writing a book. Martha looked straight at me, wide-eyed. *'Really? Are you writing a book?'* she asked, with astonishment and wonder. *'What is it about?'* Well … How could I explain that to a seven-year-old child?[98] I told her that the book is about how children can have far more fun by discovering how to play together in the best possible way. She looked surprised. *'A book about playing together!'* When I was driving home, I realized that the metaphor of play is actually quite powerful because you can also look at each of the building blocks of the High Impact Teaming model in that way. Safe Teaming is about how Martha and her friends can make it safe for everyone to speak up, for example, when something is bothering them during the game. Organizing is about learning to change the rules of the game together, if it helps to have more fun. But what is Visioning about? In essence, Visioning is about agreeing together on what game you want to play and why. This chapter answers three questions about Visioning. What are the three levels of Visioning? How do you approach Visioning? And why is Visioning not only essential for the effectiveness of your team, but also for you as a person?

THREE LEVELS OF VISIONING

Visioning itself can be about a huge number of things; it all depends on the playing field of *the game* you are playing. Research shows that there are countless points on which you can seek agreement as a team. But it has also been demonstrated that not everything is relevant for every team at every moment in time.[99] When I go for a beer with my football mates after the match, we don't talk about politics. We all know that it will lead to fierce and unnecessary conflicts. But when it comes to the essence of our team and the game we play, it is crucial to align. Visioning helps us to win. In essence, Visioning stands or falls on making choices as a team: what are the points on which we want to find fundamental agreement and clarity, and what are the points on which we can compromise and accept vagueness or disagreement?

High Impact Teams engage in Visioning on three levels: (1) future, (2) present and (3) what they need to move from the present to the future. At each of those levels they develop shared mental models. Depending on the context, one type of mental model will be more important than the others for the effectiveness of the team.

1. FUTURE: THE DESIRED SITUATION – DEVELOPING A SHARED AMBITION

The first level of Visioning is about the future of the team. High Impact Teams succeed in creating a shared ambition, taking into account the personal ambitions of the team members and the ambition of the relevant stakeholders: what do we want to contribute to this world? What change do we want to bring about? What are our long-term goals? But Visioning at this level is not only about the distant future. Depending on the specific task the team faces, it can also be about the end of the meeting, the end of the month, or the end of the project.

Regardless of the scope of the assignment, team members who shoulder the same ambition achieve better results.[100] Climbing expeditions reach the top faster in clear weather when they can see the summit. But a common ambition does not only influence speed. It is also a beacon for the functioning of the team in other ways. It provides direction, helps the team to focus and enables them to set priorities, make plans, formulate goals and deadlines, agree on milestones, and so on. Also, a shared ambition makes it easier to trigger STEP moments. Often team members do not push the Stop button because there is no ambition or because it is not *their* ambition. Maybe there are targets, but as long as these are not linked to their own personal ambition, they tend to wait for the team leader to intervene. Without a real shared ambition, team members will not push the Stop button. Peter Senge described the effect of Visioning on this level as follows: *'People no longer play according to the rules of the game. They feel responsible for the game.'*[101] They no longer need a referee who says what's right or wrong; they have their own shared ambition to which they hold themselves and each other accountable. In addition, with a clear ambition, the quality of their STEP moments in the Evaluate phase increases. The question is no longer a general *'Are we doing well?'*, but a more specific *'How does this help us achieve our ambition?'* When the stakes are clear, the team is more likely to engage in good fights. Paul Stinckens told me how top sport teams with a shared ambition truly enjoy to kick and yell each other to a higher level during training.'

2. PRESENT: THE CURRENT SITUATION

The second level of Visioning concerns developing shared mental models about the current situation of the team. High Impact Teams do not only develop a shared image about the *To Be*, but also about the *As Is*: How are we doing? What is going on in our environment? Are we in the shit or are we all right? What are blockers that stop us, catalysts that help us and taboos that are hidden under the surface? Everyone sees other factors that may be relevant. The *As Is* is not only about the task dimension, but also about the relationship dimension and therefore about the people in the team. What are the stories of these people? What about the relationships between team members? Some teams have a shared ambition, but lack shared situational awareness. As a result, their ambition loses much of its power. After all, it is in the tension between the *As Is* and the *To Be* that there is potential for strength, drive and motivation. Peter Senge[102] calls this creative tension. Compare it with a rubber band that stretches between your thumb and index finger. Your index finger represents the future, your thumb the present.

Without the power of your thumb, the rubber would just be a piece of plastic hanging around your index finger. Also, research shows that teams without shared situational awareness perform significantly worse in difficult circumstances.[103]

3. THE BRIDGE: FROM PRESENT TO FUTURE

This third level of Visioning is about making sure that the team makes the right decisions on the path to fulfilling its ambition. Which strategic choices, plans and agreements do we as a team need to make? What is our blueprint? When stress strikes and the quantity or quality of communication drops, teams with clear, shared mental models at this level continue to function more effectively for a longer time, because the coordination within the team remains intact for longer.[104]

Four shared mental models are crucial for High Impact Teaming at the bridge level. A first shared mental model is the *shared strategy*. What strategic choices will we make to be sure we distinguish ourselves from the competition, and win in a sustainable way? The second type of shared mental model at this level concerns planning: what will the team members do and when? A *shared mental blueprint* of the path the team will take within the boundaries of its strategy. Winners have a plan, losers have an excuse.[105] A blueprint is not an overly complex document that collects dust in the manager's top drawer. It is something simple, stored in the mind of each of the team members, top of mind. A plan that helps them to travel the road in an efficient way and to switch to plan B in case of problems. A plan that gives energy because it divides a long journey into digestible stages. A third type of shared mental model is called the *transactive memory system (TMS)* in academic literature.[106] It's a shared vision of who does what and who knows what. On the one hand, this kind of shared mental model is about action. It is related to agreeing on roles and having discussions on what is expected from each role. When this is not clear, people don't do what they are supposed to do. You get situations similar to a group of toddlers playing football: everybody runs behind the ball and gets in each other's way. But the opposite is also possible. The other team attacks and nobody plays defense. On the other hand, a transactive memory system can also entail a shared vision on who has what expertise and knowledge. Knowledge and competence oriented transactive memory systems help to make active and efficient use of all expertise. It ensures that team members stop trying to know everything and start using each other as external hard drives, managing knowledge in the team far more efficiently. A fourth and final shared mental model at this level is about the larger *how do we deal with each other* question. Research refers to this as team familiarity.[107] This is the question that makes many people start shifting in their seats. *'Seriously, do we have to explain what respect means?'* Safe Teaming and Visioning overlap here. It's about building a soft frame, which I have already discussed in depth in the previous chapter.

VISIONING: HOW DO YOU DO IT?

Visioning is always a chaotic process of discussing, putting alternatives on the table, expressing preferences, disagreeing and not giving up until agreement is found. There isn't one perfect way of Visioning. The key thing is that you do it frequently and make sure you don't stop before it feels right. If you just do it once and never refresh it, your shared vision becomes some kind of dogma or universal truth for your team. Then, Visioning can become a very dangerous thing. The shared vision of a team works as a filter of some sort. It focuses the attention of the team members. If that filter is carved in stone and your context changes, you get into trouble. If it is poorly conceived and focuses the attention of team members on the wrong things, it will negatively affect team performance. Depending on the team and its context, the Visioning process will be different. This is not a methodology. Below I describe an example of one possible Visioning trajectory:

I once made the mistake of trying to build a team ambition without first surfacing the individual ambitions of the team members. In an hour and a half the team developed a beautiful and ambitious story, on paper. They were so proud. Then I asked them who wanted to give up his or her current job to work towards the shared ambition. No one. Visioning at the level of the future is not about co-creating fantasies. Team ambitions either reflect things that are truly cherished by the individuals in the team, or the shared ambition is meaningless.

That is why I prefer to start visioning trajectories with an exercise on the individual stories of the team members. Before I get a team to think about what the shared gold medal looks like, I want them to listen to one another's personal story. How are the other team members sitting in the boat? Where do they come from and what is their personal ambition?

When I ask people to think about their personal story and then to share it with their colleagues, I frame it as something essential from the *I am the architect* mindset. From this mindset, we are all fundamentally free to write our own story (more on this mindset in Chapter 6). I compare life with a book, opened on a certain page. All pages on the left side are printed in ink. They've already been written. You can't change them. Your current values, ambitions and identity are rooted in this first part of the book. The first few pages on the right-hand side are drafted in pencil. You could erase and change them if you wanted to. All other pages are still empty. Writing your story means visualizing how you would like your story to proceed. It means thinking about how you would like to be remembered as the main character of the book. Which personal values and ambitions will you embody?

Some people are initially not happy when I ask them to use their imagination for this *my story* assignment. But research shows that people who write down and share their story are more effective.[108] A few years ago, a top management team in the consultancy business asked me to help them build a team ambition. Everyone had received the *my story* assignment some weeks before the seminar, and after dinner the team members were going to tell one another their personal stories during a fireside chat. But after dinner some senior partners indicated that they no longer felt like starting another workshop. One person mentioned that he didn't see the point in doing it. In retrospect, I think they might have been a little afraid to disclose their story and show themselves. But I pushed through, and around 9 pm everyone was sitting around the fire. I reminded everyone of one of the agreements we had made: *what happens in Vegas, stays in Vegas*. It is up to you to share your story; nobody has the right to share the stories of others.

Everyone nodded and the first one started. Frank, the CFO, had taken the exercise very seriously and told everyone about his personal ambitions, the ambitions he had with this team and how he wanted to be remembered as a manager in the company. He also talked about where those ambitions came from, about the butchery where he was raised and the personal values that his parents taught him: entrepreneurship, customer focus, and respect. It was a nice story, but it was still very careful. Fortunately, his colleagues dug a little deeper by asking daring additional questions. This was the first time Frank had shared his story and it was the first time his colleagues had asked him about it.

The second was a woman in her early fifties. She started by explaining that she would be telling them something she had been wanting to share for a while. '*You all may have noticed that I sometimes underperform. That I am absent at times when you expect me to be there. What you don't know is that I have cancer.*' You could have heard a pin drop. She went on about how she had worked hard all her life and how she wanted to continue doing so. About how she used to answer the question 'What would you like to see engraved on your tombstone?' with her personal net profit realized, a figure with lots of zeros. And about how that imaginary figure suddenly seemed so completely irrelevant to her. She talked about the way the team was working and the many things she despised about that. She talked about the impact she wanted to have on how they interacted with customers, employees and each other and how that could be the essence of her new tombstone. When she stopped talking, there was a moment of total silence ... and then applause.

Again, questions were asked. Why had she kept this a secret from the team, et cetera. The next to speak was the senior partner who had said he didn't really see the point in doing this exercise. He stood up with a small piece of paper in his left hand, looked around the room and said, '*I prepared a great speech, but after those two stories, I think I want to take a different approach.*' He folded the paper in two and just started to talk about how he was raised. Something changed in the team that evening – people who had been working together for years got to know one another at a deeper level for the very first time. Marc, the CEO, later admitted that he had had some reservations about the possible impact of the workshop, but that it had really shifted something in the way he saw his people, himself and his role in the team.

I don't do much during these *my story* sessions. Most of my work happens beforehand, in explaining why this exercise is crucial, trying to convince people to take it seriously, and in giving guiding questions and tools for them to prepare their story. Framing is key to ensure that people actually open up to share their essence. Sometimes I share three criteria for an effective personal story: Purposeful, Vulnerable and Inspirational.[109]

- *Purposeful*: good stories go somewhere. Some stories are boring and superficial because the main character does not seem to have a deeper purpose. Purpose is the organizing principle behind inspiring stories. It's *'the end that drives why you have energy for some things and not for others.'*[110]

- *Vulnerability*: good stories are real stories. Some stories don't work because they are not true. They may be true cognitively, but they are not true emotionally. Often they sound like strong platitudes, socially oriented one-liners or a series of buzzwords. Authenticity, vulnerability and emotion are missing. Stories that lack these attributes are stories in which the real personal history is hiding behind the story the narrator thinks the audience wants to hear. The key ingredient of an effective personal story is the courage to show yourself authentically; open and therefore vulnerable. How do you know whether a story is vulnerable or not? Just pay attention to the goosebumps on your skin as the voice of the narrator starts to tremble.

- *Inspirational*: good stories are inspiring stories. They challenge the audience. They trigger both a connection with the main character and the desire to engage. You won't finish a novel that doesn't do that. A novel that keeps you hooked inspires action. People want to take part in the inspiring stories they hear.

TEAM AMBITION

The next day I started the team ambition workshop with two simple but essential questions: *'What is this team's ambition?'* and *'How does this team want to be known by its employees and customers?'* I asked the team members to think about this individually for fifteen minutes and then I gave everyone a big white sheet for summarizing the result in a few key words. I noticed that two team members seemed a bit stressed: *'Who knows, others might say something completely different ...'* After fifteen minutes, I picked up the posters and put them against the walls of the conference room. Everyone was able to see how the others saw the team's ambition. It was revealing to note that each of the eight top managers had a different and sometimes even contradictory poster. It was striking that totally different terms were used. Someone used the word *advisory* as the role of the team towards other stakeholders, others talked about *controlling* ... at which point Marc choked on his coffee. From the debriefing that followed, one clear message emerged: *'We agree that we disagree, but that is not enough. Not for ourselves, not for our customers and not for our people.'* Perhaps you recognize the situation above. Or maybe you think *'Gee guys, seriously. How can you be so misaligned at that level?'* I invite you to test it with your team: at the next meeting, ask your colleagues to write down in key words what they think your team ambition is.

Visioning at the level of the team ambition is a challenge because it only works when you develop a shared vision that is sharp and speaks to each of the team members on three different levels: *what* is our gold medal? (IQ – mental intelligence), *how* do we want to be remembered? (EQ – emotional intelligence) and *why* do we do it? (SQ – spiritual intelligence).[111] Only when all three are present and aligned, will Visioning result in a deep shared commitment. That is why High Impact Teams have a shared ambition in three areas:

- **Purpose:** Why do we do it?
- **DNA:** How do we want to be seen? Who are we?
- **Gold medal:** What do we want to achieve? What does our gold medal look like?

As described above, every good story starts with an authentic purpose. It's that thing you want to fight for together. The reason you get up in the morning. The organizing principle behind everything you do together. It is not about what you do, nor about how you do it, but about the fundamental reason. Why would you want to solve that problem? Why do you think it is important? The starting point of these discussions can be found in the stories of the team members. But the end point is rarely or never to be found within the team, rather outside of it. So you'd better make sure you include the perspectives, needs and desires of your key internal and external stakeholders when Visioning.

Let me give some examples of the big ones:

- *We're in business to save our home planet* (Patagonia)
- *Embracing a better life* (imec)
- *To bring inspiration and innovation to every athlete in the world* (Nike)
- *To accelerate the world's transition to sustainable energy* (Tesla)

Descriptive, but comprehensible and gracefully written. I can already hear the critics among you thinking: *'Okay, so we have to come up with a kind of slogan that fits perfectly on the first slide of our slide deck. And the more buzzwords it contains, the more meaningful it sounds?'* Touché.

The answer to the purpose question means nothing unless two criteria are met. One, the team ambition should be fundamentally connected to the inspiring, purposeful and vulnerable stories of the individual team members. Second, unless your team ambition is reflected in the actions of your teams, it doesn't mean a thing. Purpose only means something when it is based on truth, and when it fulfills its promise in reality. If you do not succeed in matching your purpose to those two criteria, then your *purpose* is indeed likely to be just a series of hollow words and phrases. If you do succeed in doing it, your purpose will make you invincible. Or at least very resilient. You will find that it inspires and energizes both you and your external stakeholders. That it is a fundamental compass that you can use in difficult situations to keep going in the right direction and to make tough decisions. Purpose is the starting point for the answer to the following two questions: 'How do we want to be seen?' and 'What do we want to achieve?'

DNA: how do we want to be seen?

This question is situated on another level. Imagine this. At some point during your career you used to be part of a very successful team. That one team you keep referring to. Your dream team. Today, because you are retiring, your colleagues organize a goodbye party for you. As a farewell gift they asked five people to give a little speech about you and that dream team: two of the former team members, one N-1, your biggest customer and your wife or husband. All five were asked to talk about *how* they remember the people in that team and the way they worked together. What would you *hope* they'd say? What behavior or characteristics would you want them to describe?

Pick a team that matters to you. Try to visualize the team members. How do you *hope* that the key stakeholders see the people in this team and the way they work together? The answer to that question gives you some keywords. Those keywords say something about the DNA of your dream team. A dream team that you can only realize when that DNA is not in conflict with the fundamental values of the team members. I did the exercise with Marc's team. Four key clusters were summarized into their key values or their DNA: Energy, Authenticity, Open and Honest, and Impact. Those may sound like hollow buzzwords to you, but each of them was loaded with concrete behavioral anchors. They truly meant something to each of the team members. They were fundamentally connected to their personal stories. In the years that followed, Marc and his team used these four values as key criteria to evaluate everything they did. They used it to improve their presentations, to guide the teams they lead, to recruit and train new employees and to conduct performance reviews with existing ones. Today, it makes them proud that customers describe them with these four words.

Gold medal: what do we want to achieve?

A clear ambition in this area comes closest to goals and KPIs. It is this part of the team ambition that enables a team to determine those goals and KPIs. A clear ambition in this area offers an answer to the deceptively simple question *'What problem do we want to solve as a team?'* or *'What change do we want to bring about?'* It could be a certain ranking in the competition, a certain level of achievement that you set out for yourself, or a certain goal that you dream of reaching together.

The answer on the gold medal question consists of several aspects. For example, the gold medal for Marc's team was not just about sales, but also about human resources, research and development, and the environment. That's normal. But be aware, because it carries a great risk. Too many ambitions – of teams, organizations and individuals – are containers. Everything fits. Such a container ambition does not provide any direction. The most important thing about your ambition is that it creates an overview and that it stimulates people in the team to make the right choices. At every meeting, you should be able to indicate the pillar of your ambition on which progress has been made.

There are teams – especially at lower levels in the hierarchy of the organization – that refuse to participate in a team ambition exercise, because they start from the conviction that ambitions are, must be, or should be imposed from the top. They confuse goals with ambitions. A goal is what your internal or external client (that other team, the manager, et cetera) can impose. But nobody can impose an ambition and without that ambition, the goals set are meaningless or hollow milestones on the way to nothing. Of course, within most organizations, ambitions, values and the like are imposed top-down. But what do they mean without the freedom to translate them to your team? Rien, nada, not a thing.

SHARED SITUATIONAL AWARENESS

The next day of the seminar started with a situational awareness workshop. I wanted the team to compare their *To Be* team ambition with their perception of the current situation. I did so because during our time together, I had gained the impression that there were very different perceptions about the *As Is*.

There are different ways to increase shared situational awareness. You can inject perceptions from outside the team. You could ask customers and employees to give feedback. You could invite experts who really know the context and who can give clear observations and information. You could also stimulate sharing internal perceptions about the team openly, for example, by inviting the team to complete a free questionnaire based on the HIT model (www.teammirror.eu). But I decided to take a different approach. I drew a simple model on three flipcharts: a vertical relation axis and a horizontal task axis. '*Scientists who study groups always come back to the same two fundamental basic axes in group dynamics: Task and Relation. When you cross them, you get four stereotypical teams.*[112] I often use this model to make a quick scan of what kind of team I am dealing with. Today I am particularly curious about how you see this team.

I first briefly explained how the model works. You immediately feel the *relation axis* when you meet a team. You enter the room and the team just radiates warmth. They have fun and there is a high level of social cohesion. They like seeing one another. With other teams, a cold breeze hits you when you open the door. Then you know that you will have to walk on eggshells. The *task axis* is something you can *hear* in the stories team members tell each other at the coffee machine. For some teams, those stories revolve around problems, opportunities, projects, ambitions, customers, and so on. Other teams just don't seem to have anything in common to discuss. Combining those two basic axes gives four different team stereotypes:

- **Club Med teams (high relation / low task):** I am not talking about the Club Med travel organization, but about the atmosphere they purposely create on their holidays. Connection and a good atmosphere are the only things that matter. Belonging to the group is the primary driver. There is a dominant shared identity that is partly based on how the team members think they differ from people outside of the collective. But make no mistake, there are clear rules in this Club Med boat. *Rule number one:* never look too far outside of the boat. Don't worry about the competition. They have nothing to teach us. We are good. And it will only make us nervous. *Rule number two*: the customer always complains. Don't worry too much about that either. *Rule number three*: if I make a mistake, you cover up for me and the next time you are in trouble, I promise I will have your back.

- **Les Misérables (low relation / low task):** These types of teams are cold and suspicious. The focus on the shared goals and customers is completely lost. These teams feel like loose sand. Above the waterline, there may be shared tasks, but below the surface the goal of one team member is to bring the other down and vice versa. If there is one goal that we do share, it is survival, gasping for air. Dead rules and procedures are often the only things that keep these teams together. Like the ruins of a lost civilization.

- **Streber teams (low relationship / high task):** the team members have tunnel vision and there is only one thing in sight: the result. The goal is the only thing that matters and how we get there ... *'Das ist uns scheiß egal! We don't give a shit!'* If we have to push one or two people overboard, so be it. As long as it makes us faster.

- **High Impact teams (high relation / high task):** these teams combine focus on the job with attention to relationships. The boat is on track, people have fun and their noses point in the same direction. And if someone falls overboard, the others think about how they can pull him or her back on board. In High Impact teams, the distinction between the two axes is blurry. There is warmth in working together on the task, and achieving the objectives over and over again brings them closer together.

After explaining the different types of teams, I went through three steps with the team to increase shared situational awareness.

As a first step, I asked each of the team members and Marc to put a cross on three areas in the model: *'First cross: Where in the model do you think this team is currently positioned?'* I asked them to put the second cross where they thought their customers would put them, on average. For the third and final cross, I asked how they thought their employees would position them. While Marc's team was thinking about the crosses, I put three large posters of the model against the wall. When everyone was ready, I asked them to put their cross on each of the posters. When all crosses were on the posters, a number of trends, similarities and differences immediately became apparent. For example, some team members placed their *customer perception* cross in the *Club Med* quadrant; almost everyone placed the *perception of employees* cross in the *Streber* quadrant; and also not all crosses for their own *perception of the team* were placed in the *High Impact team* quadrant. Two team members had placed the team in *Les Misérables*. The logical question that immediately popped up was: *'Who's right?'* But that doesn't really matter. This is a model of perception. Perceptions are different depending on experience and personality. It's also a dynamic model. Perception can change from one moment to the next. The only thing that matters is to become aware of the situation, how the different team members see it, and to understand why they see it differently.

In a second step, I went through each of the posters with the team. The question was always the same: *'What are today's qualities and blockers that determine the current position of this team and what can we do to become a High Impact team?'* My job as the facilitator was to create an aligned overview of the current strengths and challenges of this team.

In a third and final step, I divided the team into pairs, and asked them: *'Look at these strengths and challenges. Think for a moment about whether there are any taboos left below the surface. Are there other things hindering us in achieving our ambition, things that we almost never talk about openly? These could also be things that you feel are outside of the team's circle of influence. You don't have to invent anything, but if anything comes to mind: now is your chance.'* People looked at each other in surprise. Didn't we just discuss qualities and blockers for an hour and a half? Aren't we done yet? But after a second of doubt, the seminar room started buzzing.

Not everyone feels safe to speak up in a large group. Even at the highest level. How many of your team members do you suspect have doubts, secret concerns or even hidden agendas? And what secrets do you hide from others? Why don't we just put them on the table? The answer to this question links back to the chapter on Safe Teaming. Safe Teaming plays an important role in the Visioning process. Without safety, I – or the person in front of me – will not dare to be as honest about what the gut feeling says. The result is that fundamentally important issues stay below the waterline.

After five minutes I collected the responses. Marc and his sparring partner had no new taboos to report. Sometimes team leaders are unable to see taboos in the team, because they confuse their own personal intentions of complete openness with the reality of the team. Sometimes they find it difficult because they see the presence of taboos in their team as some kind of personal failure, which ironically makes it a lot harder for team members to speak up. The following duo had something to say: there were two taboos for them. The first one they described as *Marc says: fear*. Everyone but Marc immediately started laughing. Marc looked confused. Apparently, many people in the organization were afraid to argue with Marc. The words *Marc says* were often sufficient to stop any discussion. If Marc says so, you just comply. The word *Impact* described the second taboo. You could feel the entire room tensing up; Impact was one of the team's key values. When I asked for clarification, the team indicated that they had already done many of these team sessions in the past – with other coaches – and that the long-term effects were close to none. They felt that they lacked support from Marc to implement the decisions made, as he immediately got on his high horse when they tried to do so. What followed was a fruitful discussion. Expectations were clarified and agreements made. And I gave my word that we would take time to seriously prepare for implementation in the next step. I invited everyone to play devil's advocate. Don't let the team proceed until you are 100% convinced that things will change when you go back to work. The remaining pairs of team members also had further taboos to share. By the end of the situational awareness session, the team had a nice overview of team qualities, blockers, and taboos. With the taboo on *Impact* in particular, both Marc and myself were more motivated than ever to address the key issues thoroughly at the close the gap workshop.

CLOSING THE GAP

With the *To Be* and the *As Is* clarified, two important steps were taken. But the most important and creative step was yet to come: co-creating and agreeing on concrete ways to close the gap between those two. It was my responsibility to facilitate the team towards a concrete and shared blueprint, both at the team level and at the level of the individual team members.

Back to the drawing board

It is crucial to establish a clear shared mental model about the steps the team will take the moment it leaves the conference room. To get to that blueprint, there are six important steps: Focus, Driver, Domain, Brainstorm, Feedback, and Milestones / Planning / Follow-up. Some of these steps are inspired by the Sociocracy 3.0 philosophy:[113]

1. **Focus:** Many teams end up with nothing concrete, because they just want to do too much at once. A lot of input about qualities, blockers, and taboos was hanging on the walls of the seminar room. I gave each of the team members a marker and a very specific assignment: '*You cannot do everything at once. The goal is to choose and work out one or two points today. Points that you think will have the most impact towards your collective ambition. Everyone has three votes. You can assign them to any topic we discussed. But if one thing stands out for you, you can put all three of your votes on that. Let the organized chaos begin.*' Everyone was walking around simultaneously marking their focus points. The *Marc says: fear* taboo and the *no open feedback culture* blocker got the most votes. The team decided to focus on improving the open feedback culture and to consider the *Marc says: fear* taboo as part of it. The agenda for the coming months was hanging against the wall, but the choice for today was made.

2. **Driver:** When teams start co-creating action plans for focus points such as *feedback culture*, they tend to go for quick fixes and obvious ideas. For example, creating a feedback culture by organizing recurrent feedback meetings. They plan for doing different things, not for doing things differently. As such, they forget to think about some really important things: why are we doing it? What's our key driver behind it? How does our plan connect to this driver? Will those organized feedback moments ultimately lead to a culture in which it is normal to give each other open and honest feedback spontaneously? They tend to lose sight of the end point. Sometimes they even create plans that don't address their fundamental driver. That's why I always ask the team to clarify the driver behind the challenge.

3. **Domain:** Once it is clear what the driver is, I ask the team to reflect on the definition of the work domain. What is the scope? I want them to describe the essence of the problem, but also to describe any of the sub-problems. In this step, I also ask the team to think about the resources that are necessary and available to close the gap, important stakeholders,

quality requirements that should be met, and boundaries that should not be crossed. Sometimes I even reach the point where we clarify a timing, an evaluation frequency and clear evaluation criteria.[114] How and at what times will we look back to see if the plan that we develop today actually works?

4. **Brainstorm:** To increase interaction and the number of ideas, I divide the group into one or more subgroups of three to five people and set them the assignment to think as openly as possible about how they could achieve the driver within the defined domain. I also usually ask them to brainstorm individually first. Research shows that this produces more involvement and more ideas, and that there is a proven relationship between the number of ideas and the number of qualitative ideas. The subgroups can come up with suggestions for:

   - *Concrete small steps* (quick wins)
   - *Agreements* (team habits)
   - *Structural innovations* (such as new products, evaluation systems, new roles, recruitment, meetings)
   - *Projects* (these are larger ideas that need to be worked out and / or rolled out with a small subgroup)

5. **Feedback and Selection:** At the end of the brainstorming phase, I ask each subgroup to select a maximum of three ideas to sell to the rest of the team. I then explicitly ask the rest of the team to step into the role of devil's advocate and provide feedback on feasibility and impact. To what extent does this bring us closer to our team ambition? After the feedback round, a number of ideas are selected. Sometimes it is worthwhile to also ask for feedback and suggestions from neutral people outside of the team. If you suggest this, some people will shout: *'No, our ideas are not finished, we will have to rework everything, we will look foolish, et cetera.'* My advice? Explain the why and give them a little push. They are just afraid to leave their comfort zone and learn. Probably, they will thank you later on.

6. **Milestones, Planning and Follow-up:** Not everything can be realized immediately. The next phase is to divide the road into milestones, to plan who will do what by when, and to make sure follow-up is guaranteed. Follow-up is crucial. Work from the mindset that you are conducting an experiment. Every iteration round serves to change and optimize things. If the idea proves to be a really poor one, no problem. You conducted

an interesting experiment that provided the team with important information: it really doesn't work. But here I am jumping ahead into the next chapter, Organizing.

Sometimes it is just not possible or necessary to complete each of the six steps. But at the very least, make sure you cover the last steps: reach 100 percent clarity about who is responsible, what the mandate is, and at what points progress will be monitored.

Marc's team had a clear vision on the collective *To Be* and on the shared *As Is*. But the final phase, building blueprints of the road between *As Is* and *To Be*, was crucial in order to ensure a real impact. It was in this last phase that the discussions became specific. That's where the team failed in previous Visioning efforts. Team members kept communicating in vague terms or metaphors. As a result, they overestimated how well they all understood one another and wrongly assumed that they agreed. In academic literature, that's called the *Illusion of Transparency* effect.[115] Avoiding this effect requires considerable discipline in sustaining the conversation to the end, until the agreements reached are solid and clear to everyone. That's something I realize every time I tell my partner '*I'll do that later!*' And then after five minutes, my partner asks when it will finally happen …

To conclude the day, I asked the following two questions: '*How do we bring this home? How do we ensure that we communicate clearly about this ambition and the shared plans as one team and with one voice?*' Often, a team returns from an ambition workshop and people in their environment ask what it was like. One of the worst things that can happen is that team members start sharing completely different messages about a session that was actually meant to come up with a shared direction. '*They spend a whole offsite on creating a shared ambition and a shared plan, but they come back and all say something different.*' What you communicate about the session and the way you communicate about it should be aligned. But on top of that, you need to make sure that people around the team who intrinsically want to go in the same direction are inspired by your messages to get (back) on the boat.

Individual commitments

The six blueprinting steps help you to develop a clear shared image of what you are going to do to close the gap between *As Is* and *To Be*. But without a specific translation of that shared plan into a shared mental model about what the individuals in the team are going to change, it all means nothing. Because in the end *the team* will not change. Individuals change. For that reason, I usually include an individual feedback workshop in any visioning cycle.

In Marc's team, I decided to do a workshop where every individual would receive feedback on how he or she could develop to better contribute to the shared ambition. To start off, I asked Marc to leave the room. I asked the team to answer three questions.[116] (1) What is Marc's greatest personal quality in the light of this team and its team ambition? (2) What is his greatest personal challenge in this team? (3) How can we support Marc to tackle his personal challenge? I asked Marc to answer exactly the same questions for himself while waiting outside. (1) What is my greatest personal quality in this team, in achieving the team's ambition? (2) What is my greatest personal challenge in this team? and (3) How can my team support me in tackling this personal challenge? After fifteen minutes, the team completed the assignment and I called Marc back in. He was visibly nervous and sat down to listen to the messenger from the team. I intervened. '*Marc, you go first. When the messenger from the team presents first, people tend to adjust their message to the message of the team. The other way around, it's not possible. I guarantee that everything that has been said will get to you in the same way.*' I will not elaborate on the feedback that Marc received, but I can tell you one thing. While Marc was presenting his answers, the nervous looks in the team became softer. People started to smile and laugh. Although Marc had the idea that he was really opening up and sharing something he had just realized for the first time, his answers were 100% in line with the answers of the team. After the messenger had done his job, Marc was visibly moved. So was the team and so was I. After Marc, another team member went outside, and after everyone had received feedback we had a clear shared view of who would work on which challenge and how they would support one another.

REFRESH

The ancient Greeks knew it: *panta rhei*. Everything flows, everything is changing. The same is true for teams. Every form of alignment is temporary since the context, the team, and the individuals within the team are constantly in motion. That shared vision about the future, the present and the bridge between the two is never set for infinity. With every step a team takes, the horizon changes. Sometimes you start with a clear shared ambition and lots of enthusiasm, but a changing context requires you to adapt. Sometimes a new team member joins the team, so the shared ambition of last year is no longer shared by the entire team. Sometimes the change is within some of the individual team members. If you're lucky, team members are open on why they are no longer running at full speed. But often it is not that explicit, you just feel it in your gut when they are no longer saying *yes* wholeheartedly. Usually, a first signal is that people stop adhering to agreements made. The natural response is then: organize differently. Make new agreements. I don't have to tell you that re-Organizing is just a shallow cover-up in those situations. It will not solve the underlying problem.

At such a moment, it is crucial that you have the courage to push the *refresh* button. *Slow down to go faster together*. Organize a STEP moment. In particular, it may seem odd for teams with short lifecycles to use the limited time you have to discuss or refresh the shared ambition of those around the table. But never underestimate the power of visioning. Even if it is just for a small meeting. By realigning the ambition towards something that you all desire and believe in, motivation is rebooted. You will suddenly notice how people start smiling and running again. The most important question is if you have the guts to put your feelings and those of others on the table, and openly discuss the issue: why are we sitting in this boat? What do we want to get out of it? Dare to be honest. Why? All time and energy invested in the wrong direction is a sunk cost.

DAILY FULFILLMENT

Hugh is 47 years old and a successful top manager in a very profitable software company. He has just reached the conclusion that the best moments in his career were the days when he was working as a programmer. He remembers times when he and his colleagues were programming until late at night to solve practical problems. But that time lies far behind him. He has never really enjoyed being a manager. In the eyes of the outside world, he has a fantastic career, but it doesn't feel that way to him.

Just as Safe Teaming leads to the fundamental value of authentic connection, Visioning also has a more fundamental value: daily fulfillment.

A lot of people nowadays lack meaning and fulfillment in their job. Consider Hugh in the example above. He is constantly among people, but he feels completely alone. He drags himself out of bed every morning to do a job that does not give him energy. He has no deeper reason. He stays in the job for superficial reasons, such as security, image, and money. It wears him out. He feels overworked. On the verge of burnout. But burnout is not primarily the result of an overcrowded agenda. Rather, it is the result of a lack of fulfillment.

You never know in advance whether you will fit in a certain team, but when it fits, you feel it. You feel that what you do means something to you. The work that you do is not just about filling your bank account, it's helping you to become who you are. You feel it when a team gives you the opportunity to make progress on your personal ambitions. You feel it when you work with people who share your DNA. Take a look around. Look at your own team. How does that work for you? Which of the team members would choose to stay on the team if he or she won the lottery? Would you stay? If the answer to that question is no, it is because other things are fundamentally more important to you. Maybe it's about projects you never dared to start. Maybe it's about spending more time with your family. Or maybe you don't really know what you want. You just know that you don't want this any longer. Fulfillment is not contradictory to making sacrifices from time to time. Fulfillment and a difficult or uncomfortable life can certainly go hand in hand. *'Some people will say that the times when they felt most fulfilled were times when they had the least, when life was a struggle. They were doing what was important to them – things that claimed their passion and commitment. There in the midst of scarcity, life was abundant.'*[117]

Visioning can be about very practical and concrete matters. But in its most powerful form, Visioning is about finding fundamental connectedness from meaning and fulfillment. Aligning ambitions so that you can focus on the things that really matter to you, together with your team. Writing a shared story together in which drive and DNA meet. Discovering why you all get up every morning. The skeptic speaks: *'That sounds quite immature and naive! Who still believes in finding fulfillment? In achieving ideals?'* I don't think those skeptics understand the concept of fulfillment in the same way as I do. Fulfillment is not something you can achieve or have.

It is disillusioning to try to capture fulfillment.
'Having' fulfillment is like trying to bottle daylight.

– KIMSEY-HOUSE, KIMSEY-HOUSE, SANDAHL &
WHITWORTH[118]

Fulfillment only exists here and now. It's a feeling. A feeling that you get while you are lying in bed at night, looking back on a day in which you did things that fundamentally mattered to you. A day in which you made decisions that were 100% in line with what you find important: your personal values and ambitions. A feeling that suddenly hits you in the heat of the moment. A feeling that you have left the safe trenches of the battlefield to run along the frontline of your life.

Teams that develop a true shared ambition are a *context* for fulfillment. No guarantee. Just a context in which fulfillment is more likely to grow. And what if the Visioning process leads you to the conclusion that you will probably not find fulfillment in or with this team? That the others want fundamentally different things? The choice is yours. Either you keep on rushing through a life that is not really yours, or you start looking for another team. What would I do? Well, that's for me to know and for you to find out. But I am convinced of three things. One. Your story and identity are not only written by things that you do; they are co-authored by the people you surround yourself with. Two. The world is big enough for everyone. I truly believe that there are others who think and dream along the same lines as you do. It's just a matter of time before you find them. Three. Above all, I believe that it is ultimately your responsibility to find fulfillment. It's not the responsibility of others. As with authenticity, fulfillment is a choice. You are the starting point. You are the architect of your environment for success. Or not.

CHAPTER 5
ORGANIZING

Visioning is crucial in ensuring that the ship sails in the right direction. Organizing is about the concrete implementation of the shared vision in the here and now. It is about how you organize the ship, so that you sail in the most effective way possible. You do that by setting up the right procedures, methods, systems and structures. Some elements of the organization are physical and observable: the aerodynamics of the bow, the layout of the cabin and the quality of the engine. Other elements are in the way the crew works together: the division of roles on the ship, the work schedules, et cetera.

Organization, in whatever form, is there to help us, not hinder us. The organization of a team is like the bars on the stave of a musical score. The bars divide the piece of music into small sections. They provide an overview and help to keep the pace and rhythm. They help musicians to play together synchronously. But it's not about the measuring bars, it's about the music. Something comparable happens in High Impact Teams: Organizing is the means, not the goal. High Impact Teaming is not about setting up beautiful ways of organizing a team, it's about achieving sustainable results. High Impact Teams realize this. They have the courage to regularly think about how they can organize and reorganize themselves as optimally as possible in order to achieve their goals.

If I write about Organizing here, it's not about the broader procedures, methods, systems and structures in *the organization* or *the company*. This chapter is not about the organizational elements that are set up outside the team, such as accounting rules, legislation, steering systems and the like. Teams often have only limited impact on these issues. It's about organizing within the playing field that the team negotiates with its context, about creating the space to choose and adapt its own way of working, structures, systems. Organize within your circle of influence, no matter how big or small it may be.

The foundation for Organizing is autonomy. High Impact Teaming stands or falls with the space the team has to organize itself in the most effective way. And don't worry, I'm not talking about uncontrolled freedom. It's not about doing what you want, anarchy, chaos, and so on. Some managers or leaders experience internal panic attacks in response to the word *autonomy*. They associate autonomy with the dissipation of all organization and therefore with the loss of control. They should not worry, because autonomy is not about unbridled freedom. Autonomy means that you make your own laws and then follow them in a disciplined manner. Immanuel Kant integrated this view on autonomy in his philosophy. Around the age of 40, he began to lead an extremely orderly and regulated – almost mechanical – life. Virtually every minute was planned:´ *Getting up, drinking coffee, writing, giving lectures, eating, taking a walk, everything had its set time, and the neighbors knew precisely that the time was 3:30 P.M. when Kant stepped outside his door with his gray coat and the Spanish stick in his hand.'*[119] Some called it autism. Few people understood what it was really about. It was a choice for Kant. For him it was entirely about autonomy. We are only autonomous if we are our own legislator. Autonomy is not the enemy of organization. It is her partner. It is the foundation from which Organizing essentially starts: having an impact on the procedures, methods, structures and systems that help you realize your vision in the best possible way.

There are several reasons why teams that are organized effectively have more impact than teams that aren't. Effectively organized teams lose less energy on things that are not in line with their vision and strategy and invest more energy in team tasks that matter. They are able to use their knowledge and skills optimally.[120] A survey of service teams at Xerox Corporations[121] showed that, compared to coaching interventions, Organizing has a significantly greater effect on team self-management competencies (42 percent vs. 10 percent of the variance) and team performance (37 percent vs. 1 percent of the variance). In a team that does not make progress because the organization of the different team members or sub-teams is not aligned, the impact of a shared vision and a soft frame is exponentially smaller than in a well-organized team. In other words, even if you apply everything I have described so far in this book perfectly, the effect will be minimal if your team is poorly organized. In this chapter, I discuss the dimensions on which you can organize, why it is sometimes difficult, four design principles for Organizing, and the reason it is also fundamentally useful for you as an individual to organize your team.

In the same way that you can do Visioning on different levels, you can also organize on different dimensions. Every action you take is, to a certain extent, intuitive. Organizing is about being able to evolve as a team from 'hoping to do the right thing' to 'trusting you will'.[122] You can do that by setting up procedures, methods, structures and systems in different areas. Below I list a number of dimensions for Organizing. That list is certainly not exhaustive. Consider it as a kind of menu from which you can choose things that are relevant to you and your team.

-   Policy deployment system
-   Follow-up system
-   Project management system
-   Meeting methods
-   Governance structure
-   Team structure
-   Communication procedure
-   Structures that support learning
-   Knowledge Management System
-   Motivational System
-   Bricks & Bytes
-   ...

If you want to know more about these dimensions, you can find information in the appendix of this book (see p. 163 for recommended literature[123]). To determine at which point you should first tighten the organization of your team, there is one crucial criterion: Energy. High Impact Teams ensure that they tackle those elements in the organization that make the energy of the team members flow automatically towards the actual implementation of the shared vision. So the question is simple: which dimension will help us the most? Don't be tempted to get started with all kinds of *urgent* things that require energy. Make your choice by researching what is *important* to be able to give more energy and achieve more impact. And be aware that if everything is important, nothing is important.[124] First things first. Don't let the urgent distract you.

WHEN DO THINGS GO WRONG?

I often come across teams who realize very well that there is something wrong with the way they are organized. Sometimes they experience chaos because they lack organization. Others feel trapped in rigid structures and systems. They feel imprisoned. Still others feel frustrated because the way they are organized works inefficiently or even radically blocks them from achieving their ambition. All team members are in the boat with positive intentions, a shared ambition, the right competencies, a safe feeling, everyone is spending tons of energy. And yet the team does not achieve the results it aims for.

The essence is the same, time and again. The only way to close the gap between positive intentions and results is behavior. In the end, it comes down to this: each one of the dimensions above can somehow help to invest less energy and adopt the right behavior, so all team members can invest more energy and rise above themselves. But when it is so clear and simple, why do we so often fail to organize ourselves in a way that triggers the right behavior? The reasons can be diverse. Below I will discuss some of the most common ones.

PAYING TOO MUCH ATTENTION TO THE MEASUREMENT BARS

When teams start to over organize, the systems become more important than the ambition, the bars become more important than the music. Or as Ignace Van Doorselaere puts it so well: the frame becomes more important than the painting. *'The preconditions generally devour more time than the essence. The frame is now often more important than the painting. We need rules, procedures, KPIs, evaluation interviews, job descriptions and classifications. We learned it at school, and we export it. There are too many managers and intermediate layers. That is the framework. Big Company People.'* Teams that get lost in Organizing don't focus on the right behavior and the desired results. The French philosopher Jean-François Lyotard described this with the concept of *performativity*. We are so absorbed in gaining control that we lose sight of what we are trying to control.[125] He wrote about friendship, love, wonder, and so on – all things that we tend to lose when we try to control them. Exactly the same thing happens in work situations. Teams over organize and lose sight of the *why* or the *end point*. They organize to organize. The result is also that they lose the power to be open and to respond to the unexpected and the unknown. People follow the plan, whether it is correct or not.

When this happens, systems detach from reality. Goals are set so high that they overwhelm us instead of motivating us, follow-up systems get so complex that they exhaust us instead of pushing us into motion. There is nobody who can work with 78 KPIs at the same time. Simplicity is key. Am I saying that teams should be less ambitious? No, absolutely not. What I am saying is that they have to stop making plans that are unfeasible to begin with – OOPS, or the Over Optimistic Planning Syndrome. Ambition can certainly be extreme. It motivates, creates drive, makes dreams come true. But plans, structures, systems, et cetera must be feasible. If they don't provide mental peace and focus, you know that something is not right.

COPY-PASTE MENTALITY

The thing that annoys me most when it comes to Organizing is the *copy-paste* mentality that I encounter everywhere. Certain ways of organizing are posited as sacred universal truths that only work if you apply them exactly as described in the instruction manual. People turn to method fundamentalism *'But that's how it is written …'* Bullshit! The worst response to this book is to take STEP as described and just copy-paste it for your team.

To be clear, I have nothing against copying; quite the contrary! Make sure you don't reinvent the wheel. Look openly at what other teams are doing and copy what you think will work for your team. Chances are high that you can use *design thinking* for developing new products or *daily stand-ups* to exchange information. In the penultimate chapter, about context, we dig deeper into the principle of learning from others outside of the team: boundary crossing. But never automatically *paste* after the *copy*. High Impact Teams continue to think for themselves. They never just blindly take over: they test methods and adapt them to their needs. Low Impact Teams blindly implement what others are doing or what team members have done in the past, without adapting it to the current context. It is that *copy-paste* mentality that causes entire teams to suffer under the *agile* dogma of their manager or the *scrum* obsession of that one coach. Not because *agile* and *scrum* are methods that contribute nothing, but because they are applied in a *copy-paste* way. In a way that does not match the ambition of the team, the characteristics of the team members, the context of the team or the expectations of the customers. You immediately feel it when that happens. The method or structure feels like a cold glove that does not fit.

High Impact Teams realize that there is no one-size-fits-all method of organization to achieve their results in a sustainable way. On the one hand, they continue to adjust their way of working until it is internally in line with what the team members want to achieve (shared ambition), the situation they are in (situational awareness), and what their people need to close that gap in a sustainable way. What do our people need to add value again and again? What works for the people in this team and what doesn't?

On the other hand, they continue to tinker with their organization until there is a match with their external environment: their customers and what is important to them. By customers I mean both external customers – the ones who show you the money – and internal customers. For example, compare the organization in a start-up team with that of a quality team in a nuclear power plant and a sales team of an online clothing store. Start-ups should be organized in a flexible way, because they still have to develop their product and product-market fit. For the start-up, the focus is on constantly adapting to the needs of the customer. Clients of a nuclear power plant need a safe and predictable organization. And customers of an online clothing store want friendly advice and fast service. High Impact Teams organize themselves to maximize both the added value they want to offer to their environment and the internal potential of the team and its members.

COMPUTER SAYS NO!

As I have already mentioned, team autonomy is the crucial component of Organizing. For some teams, that's where the difficulty lies. They are chained. Researchers define team autonomy as *'the degree to which the team task provides the team substantial freedom, independence and discretion in scheduling work, and in determining the procedures to be used in carrying it out.*[126] Team autonomy is about the freedom that you and your team get from your environment to make your own decisions and to steer your own behavior.

If your environment does not give you the freedom to organize yourself, to experiment with other forms of work, to adjust things, et cetera, Organizing will be difficult. It means that with every change you want to make to your organization, you will have to be rebellious. And if you can't prove that your rebellion led to improvement, you are likely to get into trouble. Although a lack of freedom can be a real deal breaker, there is always a place – however little it might be – where you have the power to make changes autonomously.

There are also organizations that give their teams too much freedom. That is not really a problem, if those teams are capable of using their freedom to take responsibility and write effective laws to live by. But if that is not the case, then there is freedom but no autonomy. The larger organization has a responsibility to make sure all teams are able to work from a framework that guides their behavior. Without this framework, terms such as empowerment or self-managing teams become mirages. Structural laissez-faire in fancy wrapping paper. As I have written before, self-managing teams do not need less leadership, they need a different kind of leadership.[127]

ELEPHANTS ON A LEASH

Do you know the image of the circus elephant held captive by a rope attached to a stake in the ground? When the elephant was young, that pole effectively limited his freedom of movement. Today, the mature elephant is so large and strong that he could easily pull out the stake, but he doesn't. Some teams don't manage to organize themselves because they are being held hostage psychologically. They are autonomous in reality, but not in their heads. Often they have learned over the years that it makes no sense to take initiative and now they believe that it is really not possible. Martin Seligman[128] investigated the concept of *learned helplessness*. He showed that people behave just the same as the elephant on the stake. When our room to maneuver is restricted for long enough, we continue to behave as if we were stuck for much longer than necessary – even when the situation changes and we can actually move freely. Today, most organizations expect you to move: you are expected to take responsibility for Organizing your team. But if you have learned for years that it is not allowed, then it will take a while before you realize that the walls of your prison are not in the team, nor in the larger organization, but in your head.

A DEAL IS A DEAL, UNLESS MY PREFRONTAL CORTEX IS ON HOLIDAY

You make a clear agreement: who does what, and when. You agree on what is important and what is not. You agree on the preconditions and how you will approach the challenges. But then reality strikes with its distractions and stimuli. Two days later you notice that the others were mainly occupied with other things. Chaos. One last common reason that Organizing fails is this one: we have the courage to set up ways of working, but we lack the discipline to act on the agreed behavior. Organizing stands or falls with the capacity, integrity and motivation of team members to act as agreed upon. To comply with the agreed framework – the system, the procedure, the method, et cetera – is demanding. You can set up as many systems as you like. But if people do not demonstrate the integrity and discipline to really implement it, well, then you aren't going anywhere.

The reasons people don't keep their promises are diverse. But there is one that is independent of your organization or the personalities in your team: sometimes the bucket is full. The idea is simple: we all have a limited amount of mental capacity to draw on during the day. When it is used up, it becomes difficult to make conscious choices. You know when you come home after a busy day and start channel hopping while eating Ben & Jerry's from the tub? Unless you consciously chose to do so as an evening activity, it is probably the result of your bucket being full. In his book, *The Marshmallow Test*,[129] psychologist Walter Mischel explains how the prefrontal cortex is crucial for making well-considered judgments, deciding on the basis of long-term planning and resisting temptations. This system is not complete when you are born. It is constantly evolving and is subject to environmental influences such as alcohol, fatigue and stress. Some people have a bigger bucket than others. But every bucket overflows at some point. The effectiveness of Organizing does not only result from the agreements and systems made between the noses, but also from what happens in the mind.

ORGANIZING EFFECTIVELY?

Organizing can go wrong on many points. But there are a number of principles that you can take into account to ensure that it works for you and your team. In this section I will present four principles from which High Impact Teams organize themselves effectively.

START WITH 'WHY?' TO FOCUS ON ESSENCE

Some teams know very quickly *what* they want to achieve and *how* they want to organize themselves differently. *'I followed a SCRUM course and that is really awesome! Everyone does it!'* Effective teams also jump on those new ways of working, but never for the promised *what* or because the *how* is so sexy, innovative, and hip. They all do it from a fundamental belief in the deep connection between the *what* and the *how* of the method and their own *why*.

If you want to successfully implement a new way of working in your team – or change an old way of working – start from your own why. Consider how this new way of working is connected with the essence of your team: the expectations of your customers, the purpose of the team, the DNA of the team members. They form a filter that prevents the *bullshit* from seeping through. Effective teams organize in line with their shared vision. If you start from a good understanding of your *why*, three things will turn out differently. First of all, you and your colleagues will feel more *energy and motivation* to get started with this new way of working. Because that shared vision also contains the 'what's in it for me'. But also because the gap between the *To Be for me* and the current situation in the team is focused. Because a burning platform is created and you and your colleagues feel the desire to move. Secondly, a deeper connection with your unique *why* will ensure that you will never randomly *paste*. By making the link with your own identity and purpose, you will automatically adjust methods, structures or systems that you have neatly stolen from others to your needs. Thirdly and lastly, from your connection with the *why* you also keep focus on the essence. Of course you will regularly lose focus again in the whirlwind of action. But if you always ensure that your method is connected to your *why*, the chances of staying effective are much higher. The chances of making the last domino fall again and again and again are much higher.

FROM 'ONE SHOTS' TO 'JOURNEYS'

There are plenty of teams that want to benefit from change, but they don't want to put in the effort. Teams organize a team building and expect that a lot of things will happen on that day, which means that they will be organized differently and more efficiently immediately afterwards. They expect a kind of *car wash* for teams. Drive in dirty, drive out clean. I always ask this question: '*What is the bigger picture? Where in the journey does this event take place?*' And I will not start if there is no answer to that question. I will never start working with a team for a one-shot event. Unless it is clear how this one-shot event is part of a bigger journey that leads to impact. I take responsibility to co-create a journey towards a different way of organizing in which the different steps are connected #connectingthedots. But if I don't feel their motivation to make a journey out of it, I don't do it. Why not? Because I don't believe in the impact of one-shot events. Of course it sometimes happens that a team quickly reorganizes itself at one point. Right here and right now, because the opportunity presents itself. Low-hanging fruit with which you can easily and quickly do something. But teams don't need *me* for that.

In my experience, four things are essential to organize a solid journey for the reorganization of your team. First of all, it is important to co-create the journey with all relevant stakeholders: that other team, that top manager, that HR business partner, those impacted customers. Together it is easier to realize that there is never just one lever that you have to get moving. On the contrary, most of the time many levers have to be set in motion to generate real impact. By getting the right people around the table while designing the journey, you also increase your circle of influence in the form of a powerful coalition that is committed to ensuring that the invested energy will also pay off.[130] Secondly, it is crucial to ensure that the first and last notes are just right. You can compare it to the performance of a symphonic orchestra: the first and the last notes are the two notes that have the greatest impact. If the first note is correct, it will make you hungry for more. Make sure that you and your team can work towards concrete results quickly. Work with minimal viable products and go up the mountain guided by feasible milestones. The last note generates the feeling that you take home after the concert. Thirdly, it is crucial to create iconic moments that will capture the journey in the memory of the team and its environment. Not only do those moments create a positive story, they also contain the promise to yourself and your environment that you want to invest in the rest of the story. Fourthly, you need to look for ways to visualize progress and keep the individuals in the team accountable. Make a scoreboard that keeps track of how the team and team members are moving towards that new way of working in a very simple way. *'Kids play harder when someone keeps the score.'* The importance of a follow-up system also lies in the fact that people find it rather easy to get started, but rather difficult to keep going.

FROM PERFORMING TO EXPERIMENTING

Some teams tell themselves a story: if we start to approach it in this way, everything will be better from tomorrow onwards. They count the chickens before they hatch. As if that new way of working is almost completely implemented, just because we have mapped out the journey in that direction. Effective teams frame their journey as a learning journey of trial and error, full of experiments and feedback moments, moving out-of-comfort, fast forwarding, refuting hypotheses, testing new hypotheses, and so on. It is about building a mixed learning environment that supports the people in the team to build the new processes, get their hands dirty, and improve it themselves.

Regardless of any framework, even if you want to spontaneously start a new way of working, sell it to your team as an experiment! Discuss together how you can try it out, but don't pretend it is the silver bullet that will immediately hit its target. An experiment implies that it is not yet ready, that you can still change things about it and especially that it may also fail. It is always easier to say goodbye to an experiment than to a failed new way of collaborating. Developing a well-organized team is an exciting journey, with lots of experiments and refresh moments. Reframing a new way of working as an experiment is also a strong way to convince team members with doubts to give it a try.

THE POWER OF ANCHORING

Many Organizing efforts end up dying a silent death because they are insufficiently anchored in the habits of the individuals in the team and the broader organizational structure surrounding the team. The new system is set up, but we stop the journey early and declare the victory before that new way of working is really incorporated into our team culture.

Habits of the individuals in your team are crucial to your organization. You can set up systems and structures as much as you like. If that is not accompanied by the habit in team members of using those systems and structures, then your organization will continue to cost energy instead of saving energy. Without the development of good habits, systems will continue to feel like cold, uncomfortable gloves. Many elements from your organization turn out to be dead weight after a while. They are not *real*. These systems and procedures are not in our head, nor in our hands. They exist only on paper. Systems that have not become habits are ballast. They are like benches for rowing in a motor boat.

It is neither the system nor the structure nor the manager that makes your organization work. Ultimately, it is down to the people who may or may not develop the habits and routines to work with these systems and thereby work more consciously and effectively. The key is behavior. Autonomous people usually do not continue to use a way of working that does not feel good and costs more energy than it gives. The art of habit creation[131] is therefore an essential part of the art of organizing. To develop habits, it is important to build cues, routines, rewards, and the right context together. Try to imagine and define the *the moments of truth* together with your colleagues. On which key moments should this new way of working result in team members behaving differently? How do you imagine them to behave?

In addition to those habits, there are also other anchor points. Suppose you have developed a new division of roles in the team. The only way that this division will work in the long run is if it also becomes embedded in all the other systems that the team currently works with: reporting, evaluation systems, remuneration systems, knowledge management systems. As long as your division of work is not connected to the context, chances are that all your efforts to organize yourself differently will turn out to be as useless as a seed that falls on asphalt. Any new way of organizing will only survive if the new systems, methods, and structures connect to existing elements in the organization of the team and in the organizational elements of the wider organization. We elaborate on this topic in the penultimate chapter: Context.

BALANCE

Fundamentally, we organize ourselves and our environment for a simple reason: impact. The ultimate reason that we organize the kitchen is not for the pleasure of the chef, but for the customer's experience in the restaurant. If our systems do not contribute to this, then they are worthless. Some teams miss that focus and over organize themselves. They set up self-referential systems that seem to end up as values in themselves – Organizing for the sake of organization. Organizing should always remain the servant of Visioning. The first question is always: where do we really want to go? What is the direction of this team? How you get there always takes second place. Again, the purpose of the team never lies in the team, always outside of it. If the organization you are setting up does not serve to ensure that you implement the vision and thus serve the contact moments with customers, patients, shareholders, society, and so on, something has gone wrong somewhere. To reiterate what Ignace Van Doorselaere says, *'The frame should never become more important than the painting. What counts is that the last domino falls.'*

The ultimate importance of Organizing is impact, but just as with Safe Teaming and Visioning, there is also a personal win that is at least as important: balance. Remove the Organizing corner from the HIT model and the whole model collapses. People are not machines. We are emotional beings with dreams and fears – imperfect and fundamentally uncertain. Allow us to move freely and we quickly get ahead of ourselves. We are not always able to keep the overall picture in mind. As a result, we often make poor choices: bad for ourselves, our family, our colleagues, and our customers. Then we opt for the short-term solution instead of what matters in the long term. We certainly do this in moments of stress, when our hypothalamus narrows and we can only see that one point that lies ahead of us. The consequence of this is that we get out of balance time and time again. We become restless.

Organizing brings balance and clarity. It gives us handles and structures. If we can trust that those handles and structures are effective and therefore lead to High Impact, then we can occasionally relinquish control and simply follow. No need to make any decisions, just do what you have to do, with the assurance that you're doing the right thing. Here and now. That gives energy, focus and attention. Time management expert David Allen calls it mind like water.[132] A wonderful experience. If you don't agree, think about all the loose ends that are currently on your plate and give an honest answer to the question: how does it feel?

High Impact Organizing not only helps you to find balance at work, it also helps you to achieve good work-life balance. What does it matter if we achieve all our targets in one domain of our lives, but alienate the other important parts (our children, our partner, our body)? Beware, the essence of balance is not to achieve some kind of ultimate balance between the different domains in life. If you look at it that way, it becomes stressful to find balance. The ultimate balance does not exist. But the right systems can help you balance – as a verb – time and again.

Without proper organization, the crew experiences a storm at sea and the chaos that goes with it. To save themselves, they put pressure on one another. But doing so is like squeezing a pile of sand: eventually the sand trickles away between the cracks of your fingers. With good organization, the crew experiences balance based on the confidence that what they do is exactly what they need to do in order to make the last domino fall.

CHAPTER 6
INDIVIDUAL IMPACT

You know them – those people in your environment who swear by the statement 'There is no I in team'. As if the team is more important than its individual members. To have real impact in teams, you need at least one crucial mindset shift. This one: there may not be an I in a team, but there is one in teaming. It is the I of Individual Impact. The team does nothing. I tried something or I didn't. I did or did not keep silent when the CEO asked for feedback while he looked at the people in the meeting room.

In 2018, Mieke Koeslag-Kreunen and her colleagues[133] conducted a meta-analysis of the effect of leadership on team learning, which showed that leadership explains eighteen percent of the variation in team learning. In addition to 29 studies investigating 1999 teams that have a traditional leader, she also found seven studies, covering 499 teams, that shared leadership among the team members. Shared leadership is defined here as team members who dare to influence and guide their colleagues in order to maximize the potential of the team.[134] Koeslag-Kreunen's research clearly shows that both forms of leadership have a large and significant influence on High Impact Teaming.[135] The essence of this chapter – and this entire book – is that you can influence the effectiveness of your team, regardless of your position in the hierarchy of the organization.

This chapter is about leadership, but not in the classical sense of the word. From a classical perspective, when people talk about leadership they think of someone who has a higher position and exercises formal power or authority over subordinates. From that higher position, the leader always has something more: more responsibility, more knowledge, more ego, more charisma and self-assurance, more money, more power, et cetera. Many organizations and researchers have started to look at leadership in a radically different way – and it has nothing to do with a higher position on the hierarchical ladder. It is no longer about what you *have*, but about what you *do* and whether that has an impact on the results of your team and its context.

Does that mean that I am opposed to any form of classical, hierarchical leadership? Of course not. Hierarchical leadership can take many forms; for example, think of transformational leadership, servant leadership, transactional leadership, and empowering leadership as just some of the many leadership styles that have positive effects on individuals, teams, and organizations.[136] In some situations, hierarchical leadership is the best choice. Think of firefighters who arrive at an emergency situation. Not a second to lose. It can be great to have someone who calls the shots. Sometimes it can save lives. From my perspective, there is only one *but* to hierarchical leadership. When hierarchical leadership undermines crucial conditions for High Impact Teaming – making feedback impossible (Safe Teaming), prohibiting questioning the team's ambition (Visioning), ignoring suggestions for an improved way of working (Organizing) – then I do have a problem with hierarchical leadership.

This chapter is for every team member or team leader who wants to increase his or her positive impact. The flow of the first part of this chapter is *inside out*: having impact in a team does not start with the others, but with yourself. It starts with your behavior and more specifically with your mindset. *First lead yourself, then lead others*. In the second part, I approach it the other way around: *outside in*. High Impact Team members manage to sit on their cloud, assess the team's situation faster than others, and respond to it effectively. Inspired by the model of Rens van Loon,[137] I describe five gears which you can shift to effectively influence your team: Coach (Safe Teaming), Entrepreneur (Visioning), Manager (Organizing), Facilitator (Team Learning), and Professional (Context). In the third and final part, I bring the two directions together in the essential component for every form of positive impact, *Energy*, and its fundamental value, *Legacy*.

Dr. Robert Cialdini spent 35 years studying what you can do to make people say *yes*. His book *Influence: The Psychology of Persuasion*[138] reveals six universal principles you can use to manipulate people. Very interesting. He compares using these principles with mastering the Japanese martial art *Ju-Jitsu*. In this discipline, you defeat your opponent based on natural principles such as gravity, leverage and inertia. The idea is to use your own strength as little as possible, and to use your opponent's weight and strength instead. By making small manipulations based on the mechanical principles of the body, you can easily defeat a much stronger opponent.

Cialdini shows how you can psychologically influence people in more or less the same way. Our psyche, just like our body, behaves according to certain principles with predictable responses. That's why we can make others say *yes* easily by ensuring those predictable principles work in our favor. Maybe you are thinking that I am not talking about you, that those principles only work with your naive colleagues who tend to believe any story you tell them. Let's do the test: let me give an example for three of Cialdini's principles:

Reciprocity: *people are fundamentally driven by the desire to give back what they receive or to repay their debt.*

Sarah, that younger colleague, asks you to do something for her. She gives you the feeling that she really needs you. But you are busy and it really is too big a job, so you have to disappoint her and say '*no*'. A little later, Sarah asks you to do something else for her, something smaller. Your immediate response is *'Yes, of course, with pleasure!'* Happy you just got rid of the bad feeling that the previous *no* created. What you will never know is that Sarah didn't need the first gesture at all. You'll never know she only made that request to build up debt on your side, so that you would say *yes* to her real question.

Scarcity: *people tend to say 'yes' when they get the feeling that they will otherwise miss a unique opportunity or lose freedom of choice.*

Your colleague Simon was appointed to recruit a new colleague for the team. At the staff meeting, he proposes three CVs and informs you that, due to scarcity and the high demand for people with the profile, there is a tough *war for talent* going on. All three candidates are invited for an interview. The first two candidates really don't appeal to you. Compared to those two, the third, Thomas, is a unique profile. But still, you're doubting. He is not entirely what you are looking for. After the interview, Simon tells you that Thomas mentioned that he has an appointment with a competitor tomorrow. That's it. You decide. *'Yes, Thomas will be our new colleague.'* What you will never know is that Simon really wanted Thomas to get the job from the start. He withheld three CVs similar to that of Thomas, but selected the two weakest candidates to emphasize the contrast, and Thomas had no interview planned with the competition at all.

Liking: *people say yes to people who look like them, who appreciate them and who – partly because of that – are considered likable.*

Your colleague Sander calls you with a specific question. He explains that he has great interest in X and that you seem to know a lot about it. He asks you whether you could tell him more about it. It is true, you are passionate about X. This phone call really flattered your ego and you are happy that Sander is also interested in X. He really is a cool guy. At one of the next team meetings, Sander mentions to the team how much you know about X. Later, he calls you to see whether you could solve a problem he has with X. It is a problem that requires a lot of work, but you are of course happy to say *'yes'*. After all, you're considered the expert. What you will never know is that Sander is not interested in X at all.

In addition to *reciprocity*, *scarcity*, and *liking*, there are a lot of other scientifically based principles for manipulating behavior: threatening with non-existent dangers; suggesting the time to decide is shorter than it actually is; indicating non-existent *standard conditions* that you really cannot deviate from; opening with an extreme proposal; instructing your secretary to send personalized birthday and new year cards, and so on.[139]

In essence, it all comes down to exactly the same thing: Impact equals Quality x Acceptance.[140] Each of these influencing techniques directly increases acceptance or reduces resistance to your proposal, regardless of its intrinsic quality.

Although these techniques might increase acceptance, there are two reasons why it is unwise to use them, especially if you plan to have a long-term professional or private relationship with someone. First, because you risk losing their loyalty and trust. The basic principles of influence only work for as long as your victims do not realize you are using them. The moment they discover that you use these kinds of principles to manipulate them, their power ceases to exist and your victims could even turn against you. Second, I always advise against using these manipulations because they're only about acceptance. In no way do they affect the quality you are offering.

THE POWER OF HIGH IMPACT MINDSETS

When people don't get the desired results, they tend to look for alternative ways to achieve their goals. They turn to management gurus to learn about behavioral techniques, they read books with tips and tricks. But trying to change your results by using behavioral techniques is far less effective than changing your mindset. Mindsets are the implicit and often unconscious glasses of prejudice through which we see the world. Stephen Covey[141] explains how mindsets work with his *see-do-get-see* model:

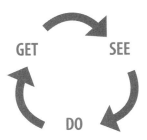

-   **See**: like the glasses on our noses, mindsets impact our perception. Our mindsets filter the reality we get to see. Things that do not fit into our mindset are filtered out, things that fit, stand out. Ever wondered why you keep seeing dogs everywhere ever since your uncle's dog attacked you? Or why you started seeing so many cars of the same brand the moment you bought yours?

- **Do**: the way we see ourselves, others and the world influences the things we do. When I think of an employee as incompetent, I start to behave completely differently compared to when I believe he or she is a winner. If my mindset is that dogs are dangerous, chances are that I will run away when I see a dog running towards me.

- **Get**: the way we see things influences what we do, and what we do determines the results we get. What will happen the moment I run away from that dog? The dog thinks, *'Nice, the human wants to play with me again,'* and before I know it, another dog is snapping at my pants. My mindset influences how I behave and as such, it determines the results I get.

- **Self-fulfilling prophecy**: mindsets tend to turn into reality – they reconfirm themselves over and over again. In 1968, sociologist Robert Merton called this phenomenon the *self-fulfilling prophecy*. If I don't believe in the skills of my employee (*see*), I will do an extra check on his or her work (*do*). Of course I will find the mistakes I am looking for, and that will reinforce my original view: *'You see: completely incompetent.'* And after I shake off that annoying dog I will prove myself right once again: *'I told you so: dogs are dangerous.'*

You can invest a lot of energy in learning behaviors that will increase the impact you and your team have. If the mindset behind your behavior does not change, none of those newly acquired skills will remain intact after your summer holidays. That's the consequence of one logical law: changes at the level of behavior can only cause lasting changes in your mindset with a lot of effort and great difficulty; changes at the level of mindset will effortlessly create long-lasting changes in your behavior.[142]

But changing your mindset is not easy. Mindsets are stubborn. People are fundamentally insecure and mindsets give them the clarity and guidance they need. As soon as mindsets are installed, we will unconsciously do everything we can to maintain them and to safeguard the support they offer. Changing your mindset hurts. You don't do it without leaving your comfort zone. It requires you to fundamentally question yourself. It calls for an environment that confronts you with a reality you don't like to see.

Does that mean that High Impact Mindsets are a *fixed trait*? Does it mean we either *have* them or we *don't*? No, not at all. You can never *be* a High Impact Team member, you can only become one time and time again. High Impact Team members distinguish themselves by questioning themselves, their mindset and their behavior. It is a continuous learning process. Below I present five HIT mindsets. Dare to confront yourself: do I think that way or not? Is that my mindset? Do I behave in line with that mindset? Be honest, nobody is watching anyway. If you don't recognize yourself in these mindsets, dare to question your current mindset. If you do, check whether key people in your environment recognize it, because **I**mpact is **Q**uality x **A**cceptance.

HIT MINDSET 1: I AM THE ARCHITECT

Archie has been working at the same bank for 35 years. He still remembers when smoking at your desk was common practice. The good old days when you had the means to really help your customers. The times when it was still permitted to make decisions based on your own experience and common sense. Today, the way of working at the bank has completely changed. Instead of having a lot of face-to-face contact, he's now obliged to refer customers to their tablets as much as possible. Instead of having the freedom to decide, he now has to leave most of the decisions to the control system. He is constantly monitored on how much profit he makes, how many customers he contacts, how often the telephone rings before he answers, et cetera. Archie is exhausted; he misses the freedom he used to have. He's just looking forward to his retirement.

Archie has developed a Low Impact Mindset. He is fundamentally convinced that his agenda is determined by his boss, the government, the control system, the customers, his wife, the weather, et cetera. He believes he has no impact. He believes his environment determines what happens. Do you have an Archie in your team? Maybe you even have an Archie boss? If this is the case, what can you do? If you want to keep, or increase, your impact, the most important thing is not to participate in this victim mindset. It may help you to gain sympathy at first, but in the long run this mindset takes energy. It shrinks your circle of influence.

High Impact Team members start from a different mindset: '*I am the architect. I am fundamentally free to choose my own behavior. And I am responsible for the consequences.*' That mindset saves you from becoming a victim of circumstances and it helps you to keep finding ways to influence those circumstances. Archie will very likely try to convince you that you are naive to think you have influence, and sometimes he will be proven correct. At some point, you may walk into your supervisor's office with an *I am the architect* mindset, and speak up, stick your neck out by giving all kinds of suggestions for approaching things differently. And maybe within five minutes you will be forced to conclude: 'I am the architect, but not this time.' It is and remains a *mindset*, not a *reality*. But I can guarantee you one thing: without this *I am the architect* mindset, you won't even consider walking into your supervisor's office. Without that mindset, you won't even try to see ways to improve yourself and your environment – even if it is possible.

If you really want to convince Archie that he is fundamentally wrong in blaming others and his circumstances for his situation, I highly recommend that you read Viktor Frankl's research. Frankl was a well-known psychiatrist who survived the Holocaust. He observed people in concentration camps and discovered that within the mass, there were some people with an *I am the architect* mindset. He describes how – in the midst of the most terrible of circumstances – they managed to keep a certain mindset that caused them to have a huge positive impact on their environment and to survive longer: *'We who lived in the concentration camps can remember the men who walked through the huts comforting others, giving away their last piece of bread. They may have been few in number, but they offer sufficient proof that everything can be taken from a man but one thing: the last of the human freedoms – to choose one's attitude in a given set of circumstances, to choose one's own way.'*[143]

HIT MINDSET 2: PEOPLE CAN GROW

Professor Dr. Carol Dweck was the first to distinguish between a growth mindset and a fixed mindset.[144] Many people tend to behave from the fixed mindset, believing that intelligence, competence, and such qualities are carved in stone. As a result, they see mistakes as something to be ashamed of, and as proof that *you don't have what it takes*. Asking questions, admitting mistakes, and so on, are seen as threatening. Constructive feedback is considered as painful or even offensive. When you think from a fixed mindset, success is all about effortlessly being better than others. It causes you to spend tons of energy on safeguarding your image at all costs (*self-enhancement*).

High Impact Team members tend to behave from the growth mindset. Consequently, they believe qualities, habits, intelligence, and competencies evolve. As a result, they tend to look for growth potential in themselves and their colleagues. They will spot it faster. Mistakes are seen as a natural part of every learning process, and not necessarily as something to be blamed for. For people who think from a growth mindset, feedback is something that benefits them. A challenge, the proof that they are leaving their comfort zone to learn. They look for feedback and challenges, instead of avoiding them. For people with a growth mindset, success is not about effortlessly doing better than others, but about giving everything you've got to be the best you can be. It's all about becoming the best version of yourself, step by step.

Research shows that people who lean towards the growth mindset on the continuum from growth mindset to fixed mindset achieve higher levels of motivation in the long run, worry less, spend more time practicing and trying, and therefore tend to end up performing better.[145] After reading this section, I bet you think of yourself as someone with a growth mindset, or at least you decide that you will start to think that way from now on. But that's not how it works. Mindsets are deeply rooted. Parts of both mindsets have already been forced upon you since early childhood. Dweck conducted experiments with toddlers and was able to show that even at that age the different mindsets can already be induced.[146] She asked a group of four year olds to choose between two options: redo an easy puzzle or try a more difficult one. Some children went for the safe option and chose to do the same, easier, puzzle over and over again. For other children, that option was unthinkable: they simply longed for the new, more difficult puzzle.

One of the factors that appeared to play an important role in the mindset these children showed is whether they were rewarded for their efforts or for their results.[147] People with a growth mindset believe that everyone is capable of growth, with passion, blood, sweat, and tears. They also believe that from your growth mindset, you can guide others in the team towards a growth mindset. Research confirms this belief. It is possible. It's not easy, but possible. Two strategies appear to be highly effective in developing growth mindsets. First, training based on principles of self-influence. You can do this by explaining the difference between the two mindsets and by supporting yourself and your team members to think *growth* as much as possible. Secondly, you can coach others towards a growth mindset by praising effort and strategy, instead of intelligence and talent.[148]

'Every once in a while Ken, that's my husband, gets a player on his team who doesn't really care about results. Or at least not the results of the team. I remember a kid a few years ago who was interested only in his own statistics and whether he received individual recognition: All-League, picture in the paper, that sort of stuff. If the team lost, he would be in a good mood as long as he was getting his points. And even when the team won, he would be unhappy if he didn't score enough.' – Patrick Lencioni, from *The Five Dysfunctions of a Team*

The talented man that Patrick Lencioni describes in his book *The Five Dysfunctions of a Team*[149] is a team member who sees the world from a win-lose mindset. Covey[150] explains in detail what this means by describing the win-win model (see figure below). This model has two axes. The vertical axis is about how much courage people show when interacting with others and taking decisions. Some people tend to show a lot of courage, others don't. The horizontal axis divides people in terms of how much consideration they show for the concerns and interests of others. Combining those two axes, you get three key mindsets: win/lose, lose/win and win/win, and one unfortunate outcome: lose/lose.

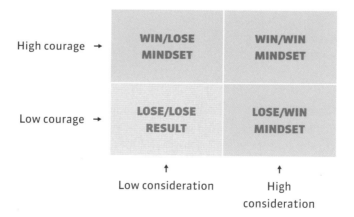

People like the player in Ken's team fundamentally think from a perspective of scarcity: there is not enough for everyone. As a result, the only way to win is if the others lose. They tend to show a lot of courage to fight for their own win, but they lack the consideration to see and fight for the win of others. This win-lose mindset makes it hard for people to collaborate in an effective way. Team members who think win-lose are so preoccupied with their own concerns, desires and passions, that they forget to stop and listen to what other team members feel, or think, or need. Their addiction to win in a universe of scarcity sometimes leads them to speed up, where they actually should be slowing down to go faster together. At a certain point, win-lose thinkers tend to find themselves running ahead of the troops. And they fool themselves with the argument that they do it for the greater good. They don't see themselves as win-lose thinkers. After all, they don't necessarily want the others to lose. They just happen to be so focused on the win that they unconsciously push others to a lose position. You could also call it a win mindset. Period.

Other people think lose-win. Lots of consideration, but insufficient courage to fight for their own win. People who think lose-win also start from the unconscious mindset that there is not enough for everyone, but their reaction is completely different. Instead of fighting for their win, they tend to sacrifice it. Both lose-win thinking and win-lose thinking can be just fine for the short term or in certain specific situations. In competitive situations, thinking win-lose really makes sense. And when you come home from a long walk and there is just one sandwich left, there's no problem with giving it away to your children even though you're hungry too. Short-term sacrifices are okay. But when you want to go for long-term collaboration, there is one universal principle in which there are no exceptions. It doesn't matter whether it concerns the relationship with your partner, your children, your team members or your dog. Any relationship that is not built on win-win will sooner or later end in lose-lose.

High Impact Team members don't think in terms of scarcity. They think in terms of abundance: win-win. They start from the mindset that there is fundamentally enough for everyone – for themselves, for their team members, for the other teams, for customers, for their competitors, for the world ... for everyone. From that mindset, they look for opportunities to make everyone's win as big as possible. High Impact Team members who assume abundance automatically have the courage to fight for their own win, but at the same time they also show empathy and consideration for the win of their colleagues. They are willing to slow down, to listen, to share visions, and to look for solutions so that everyone can contribute and everyone can win. The *win-win mindset* is the only sound basis for a long-term relationship. One last question: how many people do you need to be with in order to think win-win? Two? Three? The entire team?

One. High Impact Team members always step into the relationship with a win-win mindset: combining lots of courage and lots of consideration. Their mindset does not depend on how their colleagues or other stakeholders act or think.

HIT MINDSET 4: PEOPLE ARE SMART, CREATIVE, AND RESOURCEFUL

Imagine you are in a team of project developers, architects, and contractors responsible for building a series of apartment buildings. At one of the construction sites, a complex problem arises that you will have to solve as a team. It causes so many complications at so many levels that you need everyone to work together in order to fix it. But the experts have a hard time listening to one another. The process gets stuck. You hire an external coach, someone who has no stake in the matter. You expect him to facilitate a STEP moment to clarify both the current situation and the possibilities for moving forward, to help the team decide on the best course of action. You expect him to ask questions and listen until all the core problems and solutions are surfaced. To your surprise, something completely different happens. The facilitator arrives at the construction site with his own team, dozens of trucks full of equipment and his own plan to solve the problem. He starts to finish the building with the resources he brought. *'This will go a lot faster, don't you think?'* he shouts from his truck.

From this *answerman mindset*, you will never pull your team towards High Impact Teaming. You will either believe that you need to know all the answers in order to help your team, and play a role. Or you will fail to believe that the people in your team have something to offer, that they are smart, creative, and ingenious; instead, you will judge and see your colleagues as victims who need to be saved. Either way, you will never engage in real STEP moments. What's the use anyway? The answerman doesn't need STEP, he's got the answers. If he initiates a STEP moment, it is out of some kind of misplaced, fake form of courtesy. *'Letting people participate is really important for morale, you know.'* But the reality is that he is convinced that he already knows the answer. The result is that he goes through STEP in a very superficial way: he is not curious, doesn't ask any questions, does not listen, and so on. He is not in it to learn. He is in it to prove that he is the hero of the story. Time and time again, he fails to discover the ideas his colleagues have to offer. Simply because he is too busy judging what they are saying. And he already knows what to do anyway. High Impact Team members start from the mindset that they don't need to have all the answers, because their colleagues have answers. It makes them curious. They ask open questions and listen on a totally different level. High Impact Teaming depends on the fundamental belief that you will be amazed by how much your colleagues have to offer.[151]

HIT MINDSET 5: EVERYTHING IS CONNECTED

'Floating in space, Rusty discovered the first principles of systems thinking. But he discovered them in a way that few of us ever do – not at a rational or intellectual level but at a level of direct experience. The earth is an indivisible whole, just as each of us is an indivisible whole. (...) All boundaries, national boundaries included, are fundamentally arbitrary. We invent them and then, ironically, we find ourselves trapped within them.'

– PETER SENGE[152]

An Adam Grant podcast (TED™) describes how astronauts who return from space change psychologically.[153] They are less concerned about their own performance and pleasure, and more concerned about nature and humanity as a whole. The name of this phenomenon is the *overview effect*. By rotating around the planet every 90 minutes, astronauts physically experience that everything is interrelated. As a consequence, they develop a way of seeing things that sharply contrasts with the mindset most of us have. We tend to see the pieces instead of the whole: fragments, fields of expertise, professions, nations, et cetera. We are taught to specialize, divide, categorize, and draw boundaries from an early age. When we then try to glue the *larger whole* back together as adults, we get to see something that looks like a reflection in a cracked mirror.[154]

Some team members have impact in their team because of their subject-specific qualities: background information, experience, reliable opinions and ideas, knowledge and competencies, and so on. We tend to trust them, because their expertise helps us to make the right decisions and to achieve the desired results. Some of these professionals or experts manage to influence the team in a sustainable way, others do not. Why? Again, the essence is not in their behavior, but in their mindset.

Some team members can't see how things are fundamentally interconnected. They watch the snapshots and miss the film. As a result, they get stuck in the complexity of details and become blind to the dynamics of the larger whole. They focus on today's problems and come up with solutions that cause the problems of tomorrow. They overestimate the importance of the elements and underestimate the importance of the relationship *between* them. They overestimate the importance of their expertise and underestimate the need to connect it with the expertise of others. They get stuck on their little island. They spend all their power trying to turn the ship by rowing, instead of – from the understanding that elements are dynamically interconnected – effortlessly turning the ship with the rudder and the natural power of the undercurrent of the river.

High Impact Team members combine their passion for content with attention to the overall picture.[155] They first look at the whole and the relationships between all elements, before they zoom in on the parts. They think in terms of *systems*, which helps them to see how cause and effect are interrelated, not linearly, but in a cyclical way. They understand the relationship between process and result. They see how the process – or the way in which they collaborate with others – influences the extent to which they can convert their expertise into sustainable results and vice versa..

I would like to take a short detour here, to differentiate between work and private life in this context. High Impact Team members realize that there is only one person who moves from one context to another. Some people seem to think that they are made up of different *sub-people* who have nothing to do with each other: the *me* among family, the *me* at work, the *me* with friends, and so on. As if there are impenetrable walls between work and private life. High Impact Team members realize that those walls are fiction. They understand how life and work are fundamentally intertwined. How a problem in one part of their life is connected to or even caused by problems in the other parts. No single topic exists in isolation. Starting from the mindset that all domains of life are interconnected, High Impact Team members listen in a different way: with more empathy and more intuition. They listen to what is happening behind the walls or under the waterline.

THE GEARBOX OF HIGH IMPACT INDIVIDUALS

Imagine something goes seriously wrong in your team. The crew suddenly discovers it needs to repair the engines of the plane during the flight. Teams in such high stress situations tend to move into *Stimulus-Response* mode: work harder, talk louder, run faster. But despite the fact that they spend more energy, they don't necessarily progress faster. High Impact Team members recognize these kinds of situations and learn to respond to them in an effective way. They build in certain cues that help them to acknowledge that it is time to turn off the autopilot and to wake up, that they need to stop running and take a step back. Sit on their cloud. Unicorn was the first to refer to this process of *sitting on your cloud* as the individual **STEP**.[156] Stop - Think - Evaluate - Proceed. This individual STEP starts from self-awareness. The ability to recognize how your thoughts are racing or that your emotions are out of control, and that it is necessary to stop and take some distance (**S**top). Once you sit on your cloud, you gain perspective. From that distance, it becomes much easier to put the situation into perspective and see some out of the box options (**T**hink) – ideas other team members simply didn't see while still running at full speed. Also, it becomes much more likely that you will choose your response based on what you find truly important: your deepest values or your true vision (**E**valuate). The final part of the individual STEP is the part where you act in line with your choices, visions and values. (**P**roceed). Often, the Proceed phase requires courage and discipline.

STEP at the individual level does not have to take a lot of time. Sometimes it just takes a few seconds. But it enables you to have more positive impact. However, there is one crucial condition. What you will see sitting on your cloud depends to a very high degree on the glasses you are wearing. If you don't have the right mindset, chances are low that you will see the right things, or that you will choose the options for positive impact. In that case, it doesn't really matter whether you sit on your cloud or keep your nose to the grindstone.

FIVE KEY GEARS

STEP is the gearbox for high impact individuals because it helps them to understand the essence in their context and themselves and then to switch gears based on that. Ineffective team members or team leaders are unable to do this. They are one trick ponies, stuck in the same gear, no matter whether the road is going up or down.

Rens van Loon (2006) explains how the secret of leadership is in switching between different roles, styles and sources depending on your own strengths and the context. If the organization in your team is a mess, and you are a great manager: step up. If you are rather chaotic yourself, acknowledge who is a good organizer and support that person to do what he or she does best. Leadership is not about doing it, it is about getting it done. It is not necessarily about coaching, but it is certainly about making sure that the team is coached so the human potential can flourish. It is not necessarily about managing, but it is certainly about making sure that the team is able to work in an organized manner.

There are many possible gears for High Impact Individuals. Below, I present five gears that High Impact Individuals can switch to when the situation requires it. I chose those gears because they are closely related to both our High Impact Teaming Model and Rens van Loon's integrative leadership model: entrepreneur, manager, coach, facilitator and expert.

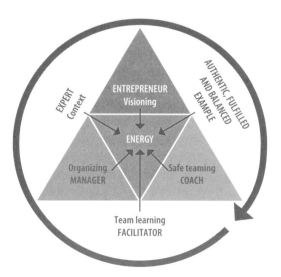

Each of the gears contributes to the energy in the team in its own specific way. The entrepreneur is especially good at bringing vision and direction, the manager in organizing and bringing structure, the coach in building safety and room for development. The facilitator is strong in spurring team learning and the expert brings his or her in-depth knowledge from the context to the table.

Most people are naturally good at at least one or two of these gears. It makes sense to develop the other ones just in case. The greatest weakness of people who are top in one gear is that they lose sight of the importance of the other ones. Remember that great visionary entrepreneur who just forgot to build an organization (manager) and overlooked the fact that his people need to feel safe in order to contribute (coach)? Again, it's always a good idea to look at your team and put the right people in the right place.

Last but not least, three of the gears are strictly functional: entrepreneur, manager, coach. They are respectively about providing direction, structure and culture to the team. The two other gears are functional as well in the sense that they bring expertise and effective conversation to the team. However, on top of that, they also bring along a certain style. The expert gear is about providing quality by sharing knowledge, pushing the point, having the answers, bringing the right facts and figures, and so on. An entrepreneur-expert knows the direction and convinces his colleagues to go this way. The facilitator gear is more about getting acceptance: asking questions, pulling, getting people involved. Combining for example the entrepreneur and expert gear, you get a person who pushes his vision top down until it is shared. Whereas the combination of the entrepreneur and the facilitator gear results in a person who pulls a shared vision bottom-up. Below, I briefly address each of the five gears.

EXPERT

Some people are experts in a certain context. They acquired knowledge within that field or context. Sometimes, experts find that the High Impact Teaming Model puts too much focus on the process and far too little on content. As usual, they are right. However, as I also discuss in the next chapter, context is key. And context is the strength of the experts. They have impact on their team because of their high quality experience and knowledge. Their greatest weapon of influence is knowing the context inside out: the job, the facts and figures, and so on. They provide the knowledge that helps the team to make the right decisions. Unbalanced experts sometimes tend to focus overly on details and content and lose sight of overview and process. Another pitfall is that they become so focused on giving answers that they forget to show vulnerability or ask coaching questions. Balanced experts have more impact compared to their unbalanced colleagues, because they see how everything is connected. It helps them to combine their tendency to provide answers and quality with the desire to ask questions to connect and create acceptance.

FACILITATOR

Effective facilitators slow the team down by asking questions with the goal to refresh, innovate and to start playing on a higher level. They support the team to really engage in STEP. Effective facilitators radiate both peace and clarity. Their steadiness creates the space and framework for the team to step back effectively. Unbalanced facilitators sometimes over-cultivate clarity. By trying to control, they over-structure the discussion. Other facilitators sometimes excessively cultivate calm and peace and become invisible. They want to pull, but the gorillas take over. Sometimes you have to be able to push the pull. Be forceful on the importance of listening to each other.

ENTREPRENEUR

Effective entrepreneurs are really good at developing a vision. From this vision they provide direction, both to themselves and their environment. They look outward, think outside the box, see the future and understand the bigger picture. From this broader framework, they become very flexible and innovative. They are not fixated on problems and roadblocks, but focus instead on opportunities. Often, the entrepreneurs in your team are the passionate drivers who have the courage to make quick decisions. *Let's move!* Unbalanced entrepreneurs over-cultivate their natural quality of vision and drive. As a result – especially when self-control diminishes because of stress, time pressure or fatigue, for example – they sometimes tend to run miles ahead of the troops. Balanced entrepreneurs, however, manage to keep thinking win-win. When expert-entrepreneurs get into stressful situations they sometimes have the tendency to over-explain and push their vision. Don't get me wrong, if the building is on fire and you know the exit, don't start organizing a brainstorm session: push! People will be grateful to you for pushing them in the right direction. But if your people are free or if you don't know the answer, it is sometimes far more effective to switch to facilitator-entrepreneur mode and build a shared vision together. Don't forget: the effectiveness of your team does not depend on the vision in your head, but on the extent to which this vision is shared within the team.

MANAGER

Managers are good at organizing. They set up procedures, methods, systems and structures to efficiently convert shared visions into results. They naturally see ways to approach things more systematically, and to bring stability and predictability, et cetera. The structure they bring saves energy, time, money and it increases the efficiency of the process. Unbalanced managers tend to over-organize and over-control. The organization they create starts to slow the team down and it costs a lot of energy. They come across as rigid, locked away in a mental prison that they built for themselves. Balanced managers think with an *I am the architect* mindset. They stay in the driving seat and continuously look for better ways to realize the vision. They make sure that systems and procedures evolve in line with the needs of the customers and the people in the team. In this way, they create autonomy instead of mental prisons, and stimulate empowerment that leads to results. Expert managers are great at consulting on structure or even driving the journey of a planned reorganization. Facilitator-managers prefer to organize together with their colleagues.

COACH

Coaches burst with empathy and appreciation. They really see and understand people. They understand their emotions, qualities, and potential. They intuitively feel what's going on below the surface, and this feeling helps them to ask the right questions. Coaches naturally appreciate people, and they understand that everything you give attention to starts to grow. Unbalanced coaches tend to overuse their capacity for empathy and appreciation. In those moments, they become *softies*. They start to confuse psychological safety with *Club Med*. They hold back their critical visions and confronting feedback, they cover up problems and avoid conflicts for the sake of harmony. *Fake it until you make it*. Unbalanced coaches lose impact. They want to make an omelet, but they are too afraid to break the eggs. Balanced coaches act from a growth mindset: they succeed in combining warmth and empathy with open and honest feedback. They stimulate a culture of team psychological safety that, in addition to warmth, also brings honesty, truth, and sincerity.

*'The secret of change is to focus all of your energy,
not on fighting the old, but on building the new.'*
– DAN MILLMAN[157]

The fundamental currency of individual impact is not time, but energy. You can define energy as the capacity to act, to do.[158]

Energy is both the crucial condition for and the essential effect of individual impact. Leadership requires you to have the right amount of energy available at the right time. Sometimes we forget that. We manage our time, but not our energy. If you really want to have impact, it is first and foremost important to take care of yourself: inside out. Make sure that you are sufficiently charged physically, mentally, emotionally, and spiritually[159] and focus on your circle of influence.[160] Have the courage to impact the things you can influence, the mental power not to worry about things you cannot influence, and the wisdom to know the difference between the two.[161] Each of the mindsets and habits that you read about in this chapter are at the center of your circle of influence. Each corner of the High Impact Teaming puzzle is within reach too. *You* are the starting point for individual impact.

Although individual impact starts from your own energy, it ends with the energy in your environment. The ultimate Key Performance Indicator is the amount of energy you *create* in your environment, not how much energy you *invest*. To create energy, there is one crucial condition: that you know what gives energy to the people in your team and what costs them energy. To find out, it is crucial that you regularly take the time to ask your colleagues some fundamental questions:

- What makes you happy?
- What are you proud of?
- What would you prefer to do if there were no restrictions whatsoever?
- What are you interested in? What fascinates you?
- How do you safeguard your physical energy?
- What gets you out of bed in the morning?

- What are your most personal values and norms?
- What are your deepest ambitions and desires?
- If there is one thing that could make your job more meaningful, what would it be?

Individual impact means that you and your colleagues discover how to create an environment that gives more energy than it costs. An environment that boosts the energy of the individual team members. An environment that focuses individual energy into shared energy to exceed all expectations. Not once, but again and again and again.

High Impact Teaming is nothing more than that: collectively investing energy to co-create more energy. Slowing down to go faster requires energy. It requires energy to engage in Safe Teaming, Visioning, and Organizing, during or in between meetings. But if you do it effectively, the process releases more energy than you invest. Safe Teaming is all about leveraging the energy of each team member by creating an environment in which everyone feels safe to be themselves, and to become the best they can be. Visioning ensures that individual energy is converted into shared energy. Like a magnifying glass focusing individual sunbeams to make fire. Organizing saves energy because effective systems ensure that the energy you invest as a team automatically flows towards the vision.

What does it all come down to? Both you and I will be gone within a few years. We won't be able to take along any of the things we collected during our life. Your house, partner, children … The only thing that will remain is your legacy. If you had sustainable impact on the world around you, your results will survive you. But profit and success are not always within your circle of influence. They also depend on the competition, coincidence, et cetera. However, what is and will always be within your circle of influence is the way you live your life. The glasses through which you look and the way you behave, your mindsets and your actions. That's what defines you today and it is what determines your legacy, long after you have died. Therefore, the most fundamental question – when it comes down to individual impact – is this one: *'How do you want to be remembered?'*

CHAPTER 7
CONTEXT

The first edition of this book did not contain this chapter on Context. That part of the High Impact Teaming model was simply not discussed. Frankly, I'm a little ashamed of that now. At the time, I tried to circumvent it in three short sentences: *'How you as a team deal with your changing environment is important and is discussed in the chapter on team learning. But I do not consider the multitude of context variables in this book. It could be material for a next best seller.'* Fortunately, I have a context of people who have a sharp tongue. After the publication of that first edition, many of them gave me feedback on the book; things they liked, but also things to improve. From the bottom of my heart, I thank each and every one of them. There was one person who pointed out the biggest flaw. Context. Or better: the lack thereof.

'You are on a plane from Amsterdam to New York. How often do you think the plane will be on course? Ninety percent of the time? Eighty percent? Seventy? The correct answer is never. If you sit by the window and glance over to the edge of the wing, you can see how restlessly the ailerons move. These serve to continuously correct the course. A thousand times per second, the autopilot calculates the deviations from the state as it is and the state as it should be and sends correction orders to the tail surfaces.' A quote from *The Art of Thinking Clearly* by Rolf Dobelli.[162] His plane is a good metaphor for your team. You are never 100% on track. It is important to constantly adjust. But that is impossible without accurate information from your context.

There are three reasons why Context is crucial for any team looking to make a positive impact. First, effective teams read their context and make it a source of information to learn and perform more effectively. The aircraft in the example pulls ever-changing information about the wind direction, wind strength, course of the aircraft, and so on from the outside inwards and adjusts constantly based on this information. Most of those corrections are done automatically, based on intelligent systems. When there is no wind, the pilot of the aircraft will have less work. When there is a storm, the need to constantly adjust will require all their energy. Effective teams, just like good pilots, realize that without information and feedback from their surroundings they are flying blind and will fail. They try to find out where in their environment the relevant information or knowledge is to be found and they develop ways to cross their boundaries. Boundary crossing is a crucial habit of effective teams. I have already discussed this in the chapter on Team Learning. As a team, you can engage in STEP moments to reflect on your own actions (intra-system learning). But High Impact Teams realize that it is just as important to have STEP moments based on information and knowledge from outside the team. They therefore ensure that the most relevant knowledge and information from their environment is drawn in (inter-system learning).[163] Some teams do this in an ad hoc way. A team member follows an occasional seminar and then updates his team during the meeting. There is nothing wrong with that. But just like modern planes, top teams build systems to automatically pull in and process relevant information. For example, they use a system of RSS readers to automatically receive those scientific publications that are relevant to their work. In addition to these effective systems, they also develop the habit of constantly driving with an open view. It is from the combination of systems and habits that they learn to understand their playing field faster and more accurately than the competition.

Context is crucial for a second reason. Effective teams develop more effective ways to influence their environment. They not only learn to attract feedback and knowledge from the context and to make internal changes accordingly, they also learn to better influence the essential aspects of their environment. In this way, they create their own environment for success, enabling them to better serve customers, students, patients.

There are a lot of variables in the environment of a team that, often without the team realizing it, work for or against it. Think about variables from the organization in which they work, such as the vision of the N+2, the organizational culture, available resources, the organizational structure, the remuneration system, et cetera. But it may just as well be about variables that go beyond the organization such as the broader culture, scientific evolutions, expectations of your customers, the legal framework of the country in which you work, the economic crisis, the strength of your competitors and suppliers, and so on. Effective teams see the essence in that web of variables. They see those variables that have the greatest impact. They use this insight to build their own environment of success by having an impact on the essential aspects of their environment.

The argument that there is no point in writing a chapter about Context, because you cannot influence the context anyway, is outright nonsense. I apologize. There are a lot of contextual variables that you can influence as a team. Think of all the people above or below the team that you relate to directly. Think of all your internal and external customers. In fact, all teams are living systems who interconnect with their environment. Especially in the context of teaming, the importance of cross-collaboration is growing every day. High Impact Teaming is therefore not just about improving the collaboration within your team, but also about improving the collaboration with the people in your environment. Visioning is, therefore, sterile if it doesn't connect with the visions of the people outside of your team. Engage in Visioning with key cross-collaborative stakeholders and get the noses pointing in the same direction. Engage in Organizing to improve the systems that support your cross-collaborative way of working. Last but not least, Safe Teaming is key in any form of cross-collaboration. If your stakeholders don't feel safe to give you and your team feedback or vice versa, this will cause problems in the long run.

A third and final reason that this chapter on Context cannot be omitted is this: in addition to being a crucial source of information and zone of influence, your context is also the ultimate jury for the quality of High Impact Teaming. If High Impact Teaming does not lead to sustainable results in your environment that are also recognized by your context, then what are we talking about? Great that we have a solid shared vision, just a pity that the customers don't want to take it ... Nice that we feel so safe together, it's only a pity that our patients do not dare to give us feedback. We flew our plane well, just a pity that we landed in the wrong airport. It is in the art of gaining the recognition of their context that effective teams differ from average teams.

In this chapter, I first map out some domains for *boundary crossing*: I divide the context of teams into different domains in which you can fish for input or influence. Secondly, I discuss how out-of-comfort contexts can serve to trigger or even compel teams to learn, and why some teams get blocked instead. I conclude this chapter with the ultimate importance of Context: Purpose.

AREAS FOR BOUNDARY CROSSING

Do you know the team effectiveness model of Fry and his colleagues?[164] It is one of the many universal formulas for effective teamwork. But this specific formula gives a crucial place to the context of the team.

The model indicates that when a team encounters problems, there is a specific order to follow in looking for the source of the cause. Interpersonal problems are at the lowest level. At the highest level is the context or the broader system. When a team doesn't work as it should, people tend to work on the lowest interpersonal level. They organize a team building to improve the atmosphere. According to the model of Fry et al, this will only help when the problems originate at that level. But if the problems on the interpersonal level are caused by problems at higher levels – such as unclear roles and procedures or conflicting goals – then your team building will be nothing more than a temporary patch on the wound. In this case, you can work on the atmosphere in the team as much as you like, but you will not help the team in a sustainable way.

As a team coach, I sometimes focus excessively on what happens within teams: relationships, motivation, roles, goals. In other words, the lower levels of the team effectiveness model. This is misguided because the problems in teams are often a result of systemic problems that are independent of the individuals in the team. In such cases, you could replace each of the individuals in the team and still come up against the same issues. But when trying to look for opportunities or causes of problems at the system level, we are often confronted with multiple variables. It's chaos out there. It's too much. And in trying to see everything, I often end up seeing nothing. Below, I have distinguished six contextual dimensions that help me to bring some order to the chaos of context. I chose these based on my experience with coaching teams and, more importantly, based on my experience with losing sight of important areas of boundary crossing. Some of these dimensions may be wide open doors for you. But if just one of them helps you to positively impact the effectiveness of your team by dealing with its context, this table is worth reading.

CONTEXT DIMENSIONS	
PRO Who are the early adopters? What do your fans expect from you and which resources are they willing to offer? What are the emerging opportunities?	**CONTRA** What can you learn from your critics and competitors and how can you deal with them in the best way? What or who are potential threats?
INTERNAL Who are the relevant internal stakeholders? How can you support each other? How can you improve cross-departmental collaboration?	**EXTERNAL** What systems, circumstances and forces beyond the boundaries of the organization impact you (suppliers, customers...), and how can you impact them? Who are the clients of your clients and what do they desire? What can you do to improve customer service and retention?
ABOVE What are the ambitions of the CEO and his team? How does management perceive your team?	**BELOW** What are the needs and desires of the people who work for you and how do they perceive your team? How can you improve work flow and cycle time?
PAST What events in the past still influence your team today? Which elements of the past need acknowledgment for people to let go? Which ones need healing? What are the elephants in the room?	**FUTURE** What does the future of this team and its environment look like? What would you like it to be? Which parts of the future are predictable and known? Which parts are VUCA?[165]

CONTEXT DIMENSIONS	
TECHNICAL	**CULTURAL**
What are the systems, policies, bricks and bytes, etc. you need to revamp in your environment?	What perceptions, beliefs, and habits influence the effectiveness of your technical environment?
How does your technical and virtual environment hinder the team's effectiveness?	To what extent do you recognize and harvest the cultural diversity in your environment?
What will it take to create a state of the art technical support system?	What are the toxic elements of the culture in your context?
What are the latest scientific developments in your fields of expertise?	What will build team and cross-functional collaboration?
What new perspective or technology can improve your product or service?	
PROFESSIONAL	**PRIVATE**
Do you know the professional history of each and every one of your colleagues?	What are the personal stories of your colleagues and your key stakeholders?
What are the skills and professional backgrounds in your team?	Are you aware of the emotional reality of the people you work with?
What is the strategic and political reality of the arena in which you work?	What are the names of the children and partners of your colleagues?

In all honesty, as a team coach I fail to deal effectively with the context of the team more often than I like to admit. I tend to be too fixated on what is going on in the team, while lots of levers are outside of the team. But even when I work with the context, I sometimes focus on the wrong levers or the wrong side of the wrong dimensions. I look for barriers in the environment (Contra), so that too little time and energy is spent on reaching the early adopters (Pro). I focus on what other stakeholders in the organization think about the way the team works (Inside), while there are enough customers and international experts at their fingertips who can provide much sharper feedback (Outside). I ask the N-1's of the top management team how they see the team and where they think the team can improve (Bottom), when it turns out to be much more important to align with the expectations of the mother company and the shareholders (Above). I focus on creating new shared ambitions (Future), while the team cannot move forward without recovering from some key traumas in the past (Past). I focus on behavior and mindset (Culture), while the structure of the organization directly punishes that behavior (Technical). I focus on the collaboration between professionals (Professional), while the essence is on the personal level (Personal). I have learned through trial and error how important and complex the team context is. That High Impact Teaming is partly about the art of taking into account the environment, seeing the essence in the complexity and then responding to it at the right time and in the right way.

WHY BOUNDARY CROSSING FAILS

High Impact Teams learn in and from their context by crossing their boundaries. But there are also teams that engage in boundary crossing and still regress instead of going forward. Below I explain why. There are three possible reasons. One: for some teams, there is either too much or too little to learn from their context. Two: some teams do not receive enough hard or soft support to learn from their environment. Three: if your team members do not look at their environment from the right mindsets, they can cross their boundaries as much as they like, it will not work.

MOVING OUT-OF-COMFORT LEADS TO LEARNING?

Some teams operate in an environment that simply feels perfectly comfortable. Their context is predictable, benevolent, structured, and calm. They experience this environment as comfortable because their basic fears – such as the fear of failure, the fear of being excluded, the fear of chaos and the fear of change – are not triggered. Occasionally, it can be nice to end up in that comfort zone, and sometimes it is even necessary for recovery. A moment of peace, stability, and structure every now and then makes people feel competent and socially appreciated. But there is one major drawback to comfortable situations: they don't trigger us to learn fundamentally.

I have to admit that, as a team, you can proactively learn within your comfort zone. But then you are usually learning within the margins of the framework that was already there: learning new skills within an existing role, learning new words in a language that you have already mastered, finding new solutions to a problem that you have already detected. It is about assimilating or incorporating new things within an existing framework. You could call it pleasant learning or, in line with Argyris and Schön's theory of single loop learning,[166] when the goal is fixed, trying to adjust our way of working to achieve that goal in a better way.

If you want to fundamentally transform with your team, it will always hurt a little. Think of double or triple loop learning[167] in which you question and change the goals and identity of your team. Transformation can also involve changing deeply ingrained habits or mindsets. And that requires – especially for the first miles – a large dose of energy that you can never generate for a long time without a burning platform. What can such a burning platform be? Feedback from your context that undeniably indicates that you are not achieving the results. Feedback from your environment about how you are perceived, or the way you work. A new idea, innovation, or change that is far from anything you have ever done. But also, a vision or dream that is so compelling that you cannot ignore it.

Fundamental learning hurts and requires a lot of energy because you have to break down or adjust existing habits and mindsets. It requires taking down existing structures without guaranteeing that the new ones will lead to success and appreciation. It comes with persistent uncertainty.

If we ever meet in a team coaching, I will probably ask at some point: 'So... moving out-of-comfort leads to learning? If you agree, raise your hand.' Usually, if I raise my hand at that moment, then almost all participants raise theirs as well. Except you, because you read this book and you know I am trying to trick you. Everyone else will raise their hand, until I show a picture of a team that is panicking. It is recognizable to everyone that this team is out-of-comfort. Yes. But is it learning? Out-of-comfort leads to learning, but only under certain circumstances (see below: Soft and Hard support). Out-of-comfort situations are crucial to kickstart fundamental team learning. But if your team ends up in the Panic Zone, it will block. The Panic Zone is a place where teams neither perform nor learn. Team members feel they are in danger. All their basic fears are triggered, resulting in emotional reflexes: acting on autopilot, fleeing, fighting, biting... The key message here is clear. Some teams don't learn because their environment doesn't encourage them to do so. Too little or too much out-of-comfort.

An out-of-comfort environment can encourage a team to learn, but only if certain conditions are met. Teams need support in order to learn from an out-of-comfort environment. There are two basic kinds of support: hard and soft support.

Hard support is about concrete and measurable support: sufficient time, money, manpower, resources, and so on. Nowadays, it is also about using existing technology (hardware and software) to do boundary crossing in an effective way. Effective teams set up (online) knowledge management systems that help them to deal more intelligently with the overload of information in their environment. Which systems could you and your team develop to better scan your environment and automatically attract relevant information? Which systems could you set up to store knowledge more efficiently and structure it in such a way that you can find the relevant information or be presented with it when you need it? Systems to improve or repel obsolete information more easily? The digital revolution is in full swing. Virtually all partnerships can benefit from getting up to speed with digital opportunities and artificial intelligence. In fact, this might be the dimension we have omitted above: virtual versus live.

Soft support is about all the things that support your team that it can neither see, nor touch. It is about the psychological safety to ask for help, give feedback and ask questions, trust, et cetera. It is about a network of people who coach and support each other. About guidance from the organization, in a step-by-step plan, clear rules and agreements, clear mutual expectations, a clear why. I have already spent enough space covering soft support in this book.

MINDSETS TURN OUT-OF-COMFORT INTO LEARNING

Last but not least, team members might not cross their boundaries, or learn when they do cross them, because of the way they see their environment. Effectively learning from an out-of-comfort environment does not only depend on the support you receive as a team. Systems also always need people who develop the right habits and think from the right mindset. It's all about the people. Ultimately, it is people who may or may not develop the habits of working with these systems. It is people who learn to do the right things at the right time. It is people who make the team work efficiently, effectively, more happily and in a more fulfilled way. If people don't adopt High Impact Mindsets, they won't turn out-of-comfort into learning.

- **I am the architect**: Many team members look at their environment and mainly see things that they cannot influence. They quickly start to feel that they are victims of their context. They focus on all those things that they cannot change and therefore they have less time to spend on the things that they *can*. High Impact Teams look at their environment and take particular note of where they can exert influence.

- **People can grow**: Many teams underestimate the growth potential of their environment in out-of-comfort situations. They do not fundamentally believe that they can change themselves, and use the same filter to look at events and other people in their environment. The result is that they consider the situation they are in as a given: *Why would we give feedback to the management team or the people of that other division if we are convinced that they will never change?* High Impact Teams believe that everyone in their environment can fundamentally change, just like they can. It helps them to influence their stakeholders and to improve the relationships they have with them.

- **Think win-win**: Low Impact Teams immediately think lose-win or win-lose in out-of-comfort situations. There is not enough for everyone so either the parties in their environment must lose or they must lose themselves. There is nothing wrong with thinking like this occasionally, especially in competitive situations. But if you always think that way – even in long-term relationships – then there is one natural law that always plays out: sooner or later you will end up in a lose-lose situation. High Impact Team members manage to face out-of-comfort situations with a win-win mindset. They have the consideration to capture the win of their stakeholders, the courage to focus and pursue their own win and the imagination to come up with alternatives that prove there is enough for everyone.

- **People are smart, creative and resourceful**: Low Impact Teams assume they own the holy grail. They are in love with their own solutions and their own people. They are not open to feedback and certainly not proactive in looking for knowledge, information and advice from their environment. High Impact Teams start from the modest idea that others have a lot to offer. They do not start by asking the question: *How do we do it?* They start by asking: *Who in our area has already done something similar, and how can we learn from it as much as possible?*

-   **Everything is connected**: In out-of-comfort situations, some teams are mainly concerned with themselves. They indulge in navel-gazing because they are unaware of how their own activities and success are fundamentally related to everything that happens around them and vice versa. High Impact Teams look down from their cloud on how the different dimensions in their environment are fundamentally intertwined with how they function as a team. They understand how the past, present and future are related. They are concerned with both pro and counter forces. They see the link between their own effectiveness and perceptions of both the top and the base, inside and out. High Impact Teams hold STEP moments in out-of-comfort situations to first clarify what the levers in the broader system are, before deciding how to deal with them.

In essence, each of the mindsets mentioned is always about the same thing: *the courage to have faith and deal with your context in a positive way*. It is about trust. In Chapter 8, I discuss this topic in depth. It is key. Without trust, people lose the confidence they need to keep on going in the face of adversity, to keep on looking on the bright side. And this has nothing to do with being naive. It is about courage. Not the lack of fear, but acting in spite of fear (inspired by Marc Twain).

PURPOSE

Purpose is a cause that is greater than ourselves. Once we find it, it is the greatest source of energy we could ever have. Without truly seeing our context, we will never find it. Because purpose is always hidden in our context.

Purpose is something truly personal, as are authentic connection, fulfillment and balance. It starts with you. But purpose cannot be found without learning in, and from context, because purpose is never self-referential. Just as words only uncover their meaning when you put them into a sentence or a story. We don't make sense until we connect the dots within our context. That's what I mean when I state that purpose is not to be found inside the team, but outside of it. There is no such thing as intrinsic purpose. Purpose is out there, where the last domino falls. In the disease we conquer, the wellbeing we restore, the poverty we erase, the problem that we solve. That is where the dots connect.

How do we find purpose in our context? In the beginning all context is random. It's a chaotic mess of disconnected dots. Noise. It pulls us out of comfort, because we just can't make sense of it. And we are sense-makers. We are hardwired to seek and find order in the mess. We instinctively try to find out how the dots connect. That's exactly how we give meaning to our context and uncover purpose.

I followed a seminar once where the trainer handed out a page with nothing but some seemingly random black dots on it. He asked us what we saw. Not a single person in the room was able to give a sensible answer. Then he showed us the next slide of his presentation. This slide showed us the exact same black dots with one little difference. Some of the dots in the middle of the figure were connected with a thin line. Suddenly, it became completely evident to all of us that the black dots in the middle of the figure looked like a cowboy on his horse. The strange thing is that even today, ten years later, when I look at that slide, it is impossible for me *not* to see the cowboy. That's how sense-making works. We connect the dots by linking our own history, mental models, memories, visions and values to the things we see in our environment. For people who have never seen a 'horse' or a 'human with a head', the dots still won't make any sense.

How do you translate connecting dots on paper to the reality of human beings? Jochanan Eynikel (2019)[168] shares a story originally written by Viktor Frankl. It's a story about an old man who visits a psychiatrist. His wife had died two years ago, and he just can't find a way to cope with her loss. He can't accept the fact that she's gone. Instead of trying to cheer him up, the psychiatrist asks the old man one simple question: *'What would have happened if you had died instead of your wife?'* *'That would have been a disaster,'* the old man replied. *'She would have suffered tremendously.'* The psychiatrist says: *'You see, you have spared her this suffering and the price you pay is the pain you feel by mourning over her loss.'* The old man got up quietly, shook the psychiatrist's hand and left the room. Suddenly there was order in the chaos, and purpose in his suffering. Random dots connected into a coherent whole that gave his suffering meaning and made it bearable. Words turned into sentences, and sentences into a story that meant something to him.

For team members it works in exactly the same way. Imagine a team member as a little cog. Somebody told this little cog *'And whatever you do, don't you EVER stop turning!'* So it keeps on turning. Do you think it turns with authentic connection, balance and fulfillment? Unlikely. Now, imagine that it's possible to zoom out. Imagine that this cog connects to other cogs in a machine, in a factory creating millions of Coronavirus vaccines. Would it make a difference?

Our desire for purpose is both one of our greatest strengths and one of our greatest weaknesses. People prefer to be part of a story, rather than living in randomness. And once they identify with the story, it becomes *their* story. These stories are so powerful that they are almost impossible to erase. Look at the dots on page 144 and try not to see a cowboy on a horse. Wizards of purpose are aware that we crave purpose, so they tell us bullshit stories. And we believe them. Not just because they are masterfully told, but also because we *want* to believe them. To be honest, most of us are willing to ignore that we are being manipulated. That someone drew some extra dots or erased some of them to make the story fit. Bullshit organizations using fancy purpose as wrapping paper.

Yes, purpose is out there. But how can you distinguish bogus purpose from the real deal? This book contains four important verbs that might help you to do so: STEP, Visioning, Organizing, and Safe teaming.

First of all, STEP back and sit on your cloud. Ask questions to help you and your colleagues lift your heads from the table. Look beyond the boundaries of the team and the first domino. Look at the people outside of the team. See the suffering, the desires, the questions of the people around you. Your families, clients, beneficiaries, patients, et cetera. It's all about the people.

Second, ask yourself and your colleagues to what extent you consider this last domino worthwhile in terms of devoting your time and thus your life to it? Does it concern an essential positive impact in your environment? Something beyond profit and loss? Something beyond winning or losing? Yes or no? A good way to check in is to observe both how you all feel about your ambition and how you all feel along the journey. Does it energize you? **Visioning for daily fulfillment.**

Third, ask yourself and your colleagues to what extent your purpose is used as the organizing principle throughout the way you work together. How is this overarching purpose translated into systems and habits? Also, do you have a concrete role that actually makes sense? Or do you have a bullshit role? How many people are told that they are building cathedrals, while they are actually just moving bricks from one place to another? How many teams over-emphasize division of labor and efficiency at the cost of meaningful work and sustainable motivation? People in brainless micro-roles are hardwired for meaning too. They are forced to erase their hardwired need for purpose. They force themselves to stay out of balance in order to keep doing their meaningless jobs. Does it matter that your job makes a difference if you have to ignore important parts of yourself in order to execute it? **Organizing for balance.**

Last but not least, ask yourself and your colleagues to what extent this purpose is truly yours. What happened in your personal history that made you connect the dots in this way? Or did someone tell you to do it that way? Does it touch you to the bone? Does it shine in your eyes and resonate in your voice? Or do you just pretend that it is yours, in order to please the people around you? **Safe teaming for authentic connection.**

We can help each other to find purpose by recognizing the importance of context, by showing each other the dots and asking each other what there is to be seen. And if your colleagues can't see anything, show them the horse and the cowboy to get the discussion going. Help each other to see how the black dots connect with yourselves and the things you truly value. High Impact Teaming means nothing if it doesn't put words into sentences to tell a story that matters.

CHAPTER 8
TRUST

Congratulations. You made it to the last chapter of this book. It is time
for a confession. There is only one thing in this book that I really know
for sure, and it is this: certainty is an illusion when it comes to teams.
Academic research is always based on qualitative case studies or quantitative
probabilities. It does not *prove* anything about that one team in which you
work.

This is exactly what you sense when you work with others – that there is
always some level of uncertainty or risk involved. You never know for sure
whether others really show themselves. Whether they are who they say they
are, want what they say they want, or will do what they say they will do.

Control is good. If it works and has a real impact. But you can't control
everything. In teams there are lots of factors that you can never control.
Therefore, Trust will always be an essential ingredient of the High Impact
Teaming mix. That is not meant to be a positive or hopeful statement. It
simply is a fact that is best not ignored. The fundamental lack of certainty
in teamwork makes *Trust* a crucial element of High Impact Teaming. This is
the reason that Trust is the concluding chapter of this book. It is the glue that
keeps all the pieces of the puzzle together.

Uncertainty and Trust are two sides of the same coin. As such, Deutsch[169] was
more than right to take risk as the starting point in his description of what
happens when you trust someone:

1. You are in a situation where the choice to trust another person can lead
   to positive or negative consequences, so you realize that there is a risk
   involved when you trust.

2. You realize that whether there will be positive or negative consequences depends on the actions of the other person.

3. You expect that you will suffer harder when the consequences are negative than you will win when the consequences are positive. The loss will be greater than the profit.

4. You are relatively certain that the other will behave in a way in which the consequences will be positive.

Deutsch created an accurate description of what happens when you decide to trust another person. But there are two problems with his description. First of all, he describes it as a largely rational process of estimating consequences. The rational component plays a role, of course. But in addition, as with psychological safety, Trust is a highly sensitive and emotional state. It sometimes even scares us because it is so sensitive. Something we do not only *realize*, but also *feel*. We *feel* it slipping away when we discover that our partner is lying to us. We *feel* it when we drop the ball and our friend is there to catch it for us. The subject of Trust is often highly emotional, personal, and fragile and we have no idea of the consequences when we explicitly address it. Paradoxically, discussing Trust also requires Trust.

The second problem is that Deutsch does not provide clarity about what Trust is. It is not that his description is fluffy or vague, on the contrary. But it does not give content to the concept of Trust. In fact, the descriptions that researchers or thinkers provide are not helpful in enabling us to fully grasp the concept.

It has repeatedly been demonstrated that people who understand Trust and are not afraid to work with it are more successful.[170] In this last chapter, I first clarify what happens in your body when you give or receive Trust, based on research by Paul Zak[171] and others.[172] Then I discuss how it makes no sense to talk about Trust without specifying the content or the subject of Trust: '*Trust in what or in who?*' At the end of this chapter, I explain how Trust fuels High Impact Teaming.[173]

What happens in your body when you Trust? Oxytocin is released.[174] Oxytocin is the hormone that gives animals the signal that they are approaching other animals. It is also called the *cuddle hormone* because it is created by positive contact such as touching, hugging, and making love. Oxytocin plays an important role in connectedness, cohesion, and attachment. In a number of scientific experiments, Professor Zak shows that people who are trusted by others produce more oxytocin, which in turn predicts that they will also give more trust to others. This can spiral upwards or downwards.

Zak[175] conducted an experiment in which he gave his test subjects ten dollars and asked them to send the money to a stranger via a computer. Both sender and receiver were part of the test design. Senders were given the choice to keep the money for themselves or to share all the money or part of it with the receiver. They knew that the receiver would receive three times the granted amount. They also knew that the receiver had the choice to keep the tripled amount to themselves, to share it with the sender, or to share a part of it. But what they didn't know beforehand was what that person on the other side would do.

The amount of money sent by the sender or returned by the receiver was used as a measure of the degree of trust or trustworthiness respectively. After all, each of the senders was confronted with the following problem: either I keep the money or I send the money and trust the unknown receiver to share it with me. Each of the receivers had a similar problem: either I keep the money, or I return the money or part of it and I show myself to be trustworthy. Just before and just after the participants took their decisions – whether or not to give or share the money – blood was taken to test how much oxytocin was released in the brain at those moments. The results were very interesting. Zak and his colleagues found that the more money people received – which in this experiment can be seen as the measure of the amount of trust they received – the more oxytocin their brains produced. What nobody expected was the following: the amount of oxytocin produced by the recipient's brain also predicted the trustworthiness and therefore how much money they would share.

Zak shows what happens in our brain when we trust people and when others show that they trust us. He found that the amount of oxytocin that our brain produces in the hypothalamus plays a crucial role. When you really want to boil it down to its physical foundation, you might be inclined to conclude that High Impact Teaming is about creating positive spirals of oxytocin in our blood, in the blood of our colleagues and in the blood of key stakeholders in our environment. However, there is one little problem with oxytocin. Other studies point out that it only makes us more trusting and trustworthy to our in-group. In contrast, the hormone tends to make us rather hostile and aggressive towards people that we consider to be part of the out-group. It fuels intergroup bias because it motivates in-group favoritism and, in some cases, out-group derogation. [176]

TRUST IN WHAT?

So far, Trust cannot be reduced to its physical dimension. It isn't just something in your blood. It is also in your head and between the noses of the people. Trust is clearly crucial for High Impact Teaming. But for me it is not just an extra corner of the High Impact Teaming puzzle. Trust itself isn't a piece of the puzzle. It is the glue that flows between all the existing pieces and ensures that they are connected and work together. Just like the oil in the gearbox of your car. Without oil everything moves more slowly, everything is difficult, everything costs a lot more energy. And in no time the motor breaks. Individual Impact, Organizing, Visioning, Safe Teaming, and Team Learning will never work without Trust. Moreover, they do not mean a thing if they don't impact Trust. But as I already mentioned, the key question remains: Trust in what?

INDIVIDUAL IMPACT

High Impact Teaming starts with the self-confidence that you are able to have an impact on your team. In the chapter about Individual Impact, I zoomed in on how impactful team members think and act differently. That impact depends on the trust you have in *yourself* and the trust *you* get from your environment. In the long run, they are connected. No individual will ever succeed in having a lasting impact without self-trust. It is hard for others to trust you if you don't trust yourself. Stephen Covey Jr. [177] compares it to a stone being thrown into a still pond. The first circle that arises creates the next and the next and the next. When you translate this to trust, the first circle originates within yourself: self-trust. This first wave creates the second wave: relational trust. Then, circle after circle, other levels of trust are built: team trust, organizational trust, societal trust, and so on. On the one hand, self-trust is about the extent to which you believe in your own character and competencies (self-confidence). However, self-trust is also about credibility. It is about the extent to which others see you as someone with integrity, positive intentions and the skills and the track record to have impact. Everything in Chapter 6: Individual Impact is about the mindsets and habits that boost self-confidence and credibility.

ORGANIZING

In Chapter 5, Organizing, I talked about how you can co-create an organization that helps your team to move towards implementing the shared vision safely and effectively. Well, you can organize all you like. If you cannot trust that your colleagues have the discipline to adhere to the agreements made, all of it means nothing. On a higher level, the link between Organizing and Trust becomes even more fundamental. If you don't trust that the systems and agreements you co-create will result in realizing the team ambition – and therefore in your team having impact – then Organizing means nothing. Organizing only creates impact and balance when you co-create rules, procedures, methods, structures, and systems that you, your team, and the environment can trust.

VISIONING

Visioning is about building shared visions that are crucial to strengthening the sustainable effectiveness of your team. Your team's vision may be as clear as a Swiss mountain lake. If that doesn't go together with the following three forms of trust, then Visioning doesn't mean a thing. One: if team members do not trust that the team has the competence to realize its vision, the shared vision loses its power. *Group potency* can be described as the shared confidence in the ability of the team to perform. It is one of the most robust predictors of team effectiveness in scientific research.[178] Two: if you cannot trust that the individuals in the team are really committed to move in the agreed direction, what does your shared ambition mean? *Task cohesion* can be described as the shared trust that the team is connected around the same tasks, goals or ambitions. In their meta-analysis of research on 1044 teams, Brian Mullen and Carolyn Copper show that task cohesion has a strong positive effect on team performance, and this is stronger than social cohesion.[179] Three: if you cannot trust that a win for one team member is also a win for the others and vice versa, then you really should ask yourself and each other whether or not you need and want to work together. *Positive interdependence* is the shared trust that team members need each other's success to achieve their goals. This form of trust is at the heart of teaming. David Johnson and Roger Johnson found 375 studies over the past hundred years that investigate the effect of positive interdependence with demonstrated positive effects on learning, productivity, retention, psychological health, and so on.[180]

SAFE TEAMING

Safe Teaming does not exist without Trust and vice versa, because Safe Teaming simply *is* a form of Trust. It is the Trust that your team is safe for socially risky behavior. The shared belief that no one gets killed for speaking up, admitting a mistake, or asking a question.

TEAM LEARNING

The High Impact Teaming Model is the foundation of this book. The underlying idea of this model is that nobody knows anything for sure and that you have to find out what works for you and what doesn't on different fronts, by slowing down to go faster.

But you will never effectively slow down to learn as a team if you do not trust that it will actually help you to accelerate. Some level of Trust in the concept of team learning is required to make it work. STEP moments become ineffective when you frame them as something negative.[181] Low trust makes your team learn slowly at a high cost and a low return on energy. High trust, on the other hand, helps the team to learn at a low cost and high return on energy.[182] When Trust is high, STEP and feedback are easy, they are self evident and they have a higher return on energy. So Trust is fundamental for High Impact Teaming.

I end this book by linking trust to the last part of the High Impact Teaming model: Context. I am aware that not everyone wants to make our planet a better place. Strategic games, self-promotion, hatred, and aggression are part of who we are as a species. One thing we can agree on: a vast number of things are incredibly messed up within our current context. How is it possible that the 42 richest people possess more than the 3.7 billion poorest?![183] How is it possible that women are still dominated by men in so many households and in so many countries?[184] How is it possible that we keep filling our seas with microplastics[185] and that we keep emitting greenhouse gases?[186] All these issues are examples of our collective destructiveness. And all of these issues are opportunities for collaboration to make it right again.

How is it possible that it has come to this? I think there are two fundamental reasons: first, something goes wrong in our minds. We seem to have an inherent capability for self-deception. In my opinion, every form of human evil is somehow linked to self-deception. We continue doing the wrong thing habitually, because our minds choose the unconscious routine over new and untrodden paths and because we are capable of lying to ourselves about the consequences of the collective actions we engage in. Even when it comes to obvious wrongdoing, like genocide or mass pollution, individuals are capable of believing what suits them. We are programmed to prefer the lie over the truth when there is a risk that the truth will threaten our self image. As a result, we deceive ourselves continuously: *'Yes, I am a good husband.' 'Of course I am a good mother.' 'Sure, I take care of my colleagues.'* After a while, we get trapped in the web of lies we have created, which form the context for new *alternative truths* and new wrongdoing. At some point, the annoying feeling that something isn't right simply disappears. We lose track of what we really believe, think, feel, or want, let alone why. We lose contact with our true selves. Self-deception is what makes perfectly good people do perfectly bad things.

The truth can't hurt you, it's just like the dark. It scares you witless, but in time you see things clear and stark.[187]

– Elvis Costello

Second, there's something wrong with the way we communicate with one another. The *Abilene paradox* illustrates quite well what I mean here.[188] Are you familiar with that paradox? It is the strange phenomenon in which all the team members agree to walk in the wrong direction for hours. When you interview them separately, it turns out that every single one of them feels or knows the team is on the wrong track. But somehow, when you put them together, they collectively decide to go in the wrong direction. How is that possible? The cause can be found both in our ability to lie to ourselves and to lie to each other. Lying is one of our key resources for social survival in a world where the truth is threatening to the (self)image of others and, as a result, is threatening to ourselves. Ego makes it so very hard to stand up for what we truly believe in, to really confront each other, to ask questions that could make us look stupid. When somebody confronts us, we take it so personally that they stop doing it. At the same time, we make assumptions about what should or should not be communicated. We assume that as the majority is silent, they agree with the chosen direction and we – the minority – must be wrong. So we keep our mouths shut and get stuck in assumptions about what the others really think and want. Where individuals are champions in self-deception and therefore often not really connected to themselves, collectives perfect the art of deception so they don't have to confront each other.

This book is about teaming, but the mechanisms I describe apply not only to teams, but also to divisions, organizations, families, societies, cultures, and perhaps even to humanity as a whole. Working together at higher levels may be more complex and more difficult to achieve. But it is not fundamentally different. The former top manager of a large mobile telecommunications company and bass player of the Belgian band *De Mens*, Michel De Coster, explains perfectly how I see it: '*Managing 50, 100, 1.000 or 5.000 people is less different than you may think. Nobody has 5.000 direct reports. Ultimately, it always comes down to working intensively with a small group of three to fifteen people.*'[189] If teams at the highest level manage to work together effectively, they become a kind of lever for the effectiveness of other teams, the entire organization, and potentially the world.

Never doubt that a small group of thoughtful, committed citizens can change the world; indeed, it's the only thing that ever has.[190]

– MARGARET MEAD

I have concluded this book with a chapter on trust. Trust that it is still possible and that others want it too. Trust that no one will look in the mirror while brushing their teeth tonight and think: *'Tomorrow I'm going to ruin the world for my children and grandchildren.'* Individual Impact, Team Learning, Safe Teaming, Visioning, and Organizing are ways to break the cycles of self-deception in our minds and to restore the connections between our hearts. It is an invitation to trust that it makes sense, that it matters, and that the others will eventually see that as well. To trust that we can build the foundations of our own collaboration ourselves. To trust that energy for High Impact Teaming leads to more trust and vice versa. Trust is the essence of every form of collaboration. The oil in the gearbox. Even in the collaboration between an author and a reader. Because without Trust, you would have stopped reading a long time ago and I would have stopped writing. Why? Because everyone doubts and no one ever knows for sure.

ENDORSEMENTS

'Stefan preaches in this book what he professed in the Unicorn sessions where I met him a few years ago: that there is no unique formula for successful leadership or for working as a team. But there is a set of tools from which you can select those you need for the context you are in. This book then, if anything, is a toolbox – that gathers and organizes those tools so that individuals, leaders and coaches across organizations can improve how they work and win together. My favorite tools in the box are the 'soft frame' and the focus on authentic connections. Combined with the notion of 'I am the Architect', the equivalent of what we call 'Ownership' at AB InBev, they have unlocked doors and made leading teams and being part of them a much more fun, inspiring and rewarding experience.'
Simon Wuestenberg | Region Vice President, Midwest US, Anheuser-Busch InBev

'This book can help leaders to become even better leaders – by helping them to understand how they can contribute to create High Impact Teaming.'
Jochen Gleisberg | Senior Partner Roland Berger

'This book is a compelling, pragmatic argument for the development of the individual as a prerequisite for successful collaboration. A must-read for leaders who want their teams to become greater than the sum of their parts.'
Lars Fahrenbach | Managing Director Vergölst

'Decuyper, Raes and Boon share their models for creating effective teams. But they take this a step further: they challenge you on how to adjust the models to your particular context, and make you start from the impact you can have as an individual.'
Annelies Missotten | Senior Vice President Human Resources Galapagos

ACKNOWLEDGMENTS

You know what's next. Thanking people.

Unicorn, more specifically Paul Stinckens and Joris Roels. For inspiring us more than anyone else. Without you, this book would never have been written. STEP on an individual level, the winning team model, and the story of the kayak are only a few of the examples that show that we're standing on the shoulders of 25 years of experience. And we have more to be thankful for. You have given us a platform to meet and coach top-level teams. Thanks to you, it has become clear to us how the gap between theory and practice is always much greater in practice than in theory, and more importantly, how you can close it. www.unicorngroup.be.

Prof. Dr. Filip Dochy. You gave us the confidence and support to do a PhD on team learning. To study and research teams, to be inspired, to become more insightful. Without you we would never have found each other and we would never have come up with the title High Impact Teaming. As such, we put ourselves back under your wings.

Veerle Vandeweyer and Anna Rich, for reading through this book with your linguistic expertise, for correcting spelling and grammar flaws.

To all our present and former employers and colleagues. Thank you for giving us the opportunity to work in and with teams. You have helped us each in your own way to better understand the phenomenon *team*.

Wilfried Massenhove and Joris Vermang, thanks for sparring about the fundamental impact of each of the three corners in the High Impact Teaming model. Wilfried, thank you for connecting us to Wilfried Neven.

Ignace Van Doorselaere. Hundreds or maybe thousands of people have been inspired by your words and acts. Thank you for welcoming us to interview you. And thanks for the amazing Neuhaus chocolates.

Wilfried Neven. You gave us a serious reality check. With your sharp mind, modesty, and openness, you enlightened us about the meaning of STEP in a working environment, and the crucial role of psychological safety in making anything work.

To all the people who gave us feedback and important insights that allowed us to improve our book: Thank you! Thanks Kwinten Fort, Emilie Schollaert, Bert Peene, Tom Spittaels, Goele Nickmans, Kathleen Vande Kerckhove, Inge Van Droogenbroeck, Toon Quaghebeur, Liesbeth Geuvens, Marie De Laet, Sofie Willox, Stéphanie Habrant, Jasper Deneut, Jelle Jacquet, Jeroen Geusens, Elise Desimpelaere, Herman Baert, Kim Schroeven, Mathieu Tallon, Geert Baro, Eva De Smedt, Stijn Smeets, Bavo Smets, Kris Meirhaeghe, Annemarie Raes, Lars Fahrenbach, Simon Wuestenberg, Annelies Missotten, Jochen Gleisberg, Matthias Nauwelaers, Lisbeth Decneut, Amy Edmondson, Annelies Wybo, Piet Van den Bossche, Catherine Gabelica and Rens Van Loon.

To our parents, families, and friends. Thank you for supporting us throughout the years, for giving us feedback, and for cheering us on while we were writing this book.

Melina, Max, and Sam. Thanks for giving us the space to do our thing, and for being there, always.

To our children, Lara, Billie, and Morris. Make it count!

APPENDIX

Policy deployment system

A policy deployment system ensures that teams in the organization translate their ambition, vision, and strategy into concrete, impactful actions. For example, they help to start from the real voice of the customer; translate the vision and strategy into a limited number of concrete breakthrough goals (3-5 years) and focus all energy on that; convert the breakthrough goals into milestones and result and action KPIs; develop the milestones and KPIs into concrete team and individual plans with specific and innovative actions and deadlines; and manage the resources in the team so that the team is able to execute the plans. The main challenge is to ensure that every action serves to cascade ambition into each of the customer's impact points.

Follow-up system

High Impact Teams have a cockpit that helps them to follow up how the team and individual team members make progress towards the team ambition. For this, they often use a KPI-based system that indicates which actions have been taken, which are on the right track and which are not. Using KPIs that only track results and fail to evaluate which actions cause the results is like driving a car and only looking in your rearview mirror. Effective follow-up systems also help to give everyone an overview of who is doing what, who has which workload and whether or not the team has the necessary resources in time, money, and people to implement the plan.

Project management system

The project management system supports the team in the way it organizes, prepares, plans, executes, documents, and concludes projects. The domains on which a team can use support from a project management system are scope, time, HR, technical resources, quality, quantity, and budget. Well-known project management systems are: evo, agile, scrum, dsdm, rup, goth, lean, prince, and many others.

Meeting method

Meetings are the heartbeat and the rhythm of your teamwork. The energy, interaction and involvement at these moments are crucial. Low Impact teams reinvent how they approach it each time or tackle each type of meeting in the same way. High Impact teams gradually develop a method to ensure that all their meetings run effectively. Basic elements are:

- preparation
- goal, agenda, and meeting plan
- rules of engagement and facilitator
- to do's, planning and follow-up system
- strong start and end note

Governance structure

To achieve results, teams must make decisions. The governance system determines which matters are decided at what times by who and how. Clarity about the governance structure ensures that it is clear where the autonomy lies for the team, the sub-teams and the team members. What can we / may I decide here and now and what can we / I not? These agreements about who decides determine who is given the mandate to make decisions. They also determine which stakeholders should be involved and to what extent people feel ownership. Making agreements about how decisions are made in different situations ensures that the team does not block if, for example, the team members disagree.

Team structure

High Impact Teams make agreements about roles and responsibilities. They do that primarily to ensure that all the important functions the team needs to perform have been covered. Team roles help the team to divide work and avoid duplication. They also help to analyze where things go wrong or what is missing. Team roles also lead to specialization and shared knowledge about the specialization. If there are clear team roles, you don't have to do and remember everything. You can transfer tasks and information.

In High Impact Teams, team roles are divided based on talents and it is made explicit what is expected from each role. But the most important thing is that every role remains connected to the whole picture at all times, just like football teams, for example. If there is an attack, the defense moves as well. When defending, the strikers fold back. Depending on the whole, the team roles are also used flexibly.

Communication procedures

High Impact Teams have solid internal and external communication procedures that ensure that they have a sustainable impact and are also recognized for it.

- At what moments do we communicate with each other and with the outside world?
- Which communication tools support our communication?
- How do we communicate with each other?
- Are we doing it in line with mutual expectations regarding style and content?
- How do we ensure that our communication is *closed loop*? That what I send is received by you in the same way I meant it?
- How do we ensure that we are perceived by our environment the way we want to be perceived?

Structure that supports learning

The theme of this book is learning. So I don't have to explain its importance any further. But a team can also organize for learning. To set up a structure that supports learning as a team, you could, for example, build in reflection moments and organize good fight sessions.

Knowledge management system

Knowledge management systems are systems to efficiently attract, store, and deploy information and knowledge in the team.

Motivation system

Without the motivation of the individual team members to work on the shared ambition, there is no real cooperation. Which tools do you use to ensure and support motivation of team members? You can support intrinsic motivation by ensuring that your team members can pursue their individual ambitions within the team. You can support extrinsic motivation by playing with reward systems, personal development of individual team members or promotions and other forms of appreciation, such as team bonuses.

Bricks & Bytes

The physical and digital working environment is a very important aspect of your organization. How do you organize them? It can be about what the work spaces look like, which online programmes you use to collaborate, where you work, how you build the canteen, where you have your team meetings, and so on.

ENDNOTES

1   Decuyper, S. (2010). *Modelling and Facilitating Team Learning*. Unpublished dissertation. Katholieke Universiteit Leuven.
Raes, E. (2015). *Team's Anatomy. Exploring Change in Teams*. Unpublished dissertation. Katholieke Universiteit Leuven.
Boon, A. (2016). *Complexity, Creativity, Teams. Exploring Task Complexity and Creative Processes in Project Teams*. Unpublished dissertation. Katholieke Universiteit Leuven.

2   All stories in this book are inspired by facts, but the names I used are not the real names of people involved.

3   Solet, D.J., Norvell, J., Rutan, G.H. & Frankel, R.M. (2012). Lost in Translation: Challenges and Opportunities in Physician-to-Physician Communication During Patient Handoffs. *Academic Medicine, 80* (12). 1094-1099.

4   Habrant, S. (2017). Op welke manier kan bedside briefing zorgen voor een betere kwaliteit op de afdeling cardiologie/vaatheelkunde? Unpublished dissertation.

5   Bedside Briefing was introduced in this hospital by a nurse in the team who got interested in the topic during her educational program. She wrote her thesis about this topic (see note 4).

6   Raes, E., Kyndt, E. & Dochy, F. (2015). Turning Points During the Life of Student Project Teams. A Qualitative Study. *Frontline Learning Research 3*(2), 63-89. doi: 10.14786/flr.v3i2.166.

7   Visited on 29/08/2018 op http://www.woorden.org/quotes/?auteur=Sören%20Kierkegaard.

8   I heard about this for the first time during an AB InBev training. I later read about it in: Lammers, M. (2015). *Yes! Een Crisis. Top Coaches*, Baarn: Tirion Sport.

9   Koeslag-Kreunen, M., Van den Bossche, P., Hoven, M., Van der Klink, M. & Gijselaers, M. (2004). When Leadership Powers Team Learning: A Meta-Analysis. *Small Group Research 49*(4), 1–39. doi: 10.1177/1046496418764824.

10   For the sake of simplicity, we will talk about teams. Remember that we use that word to refer to any form of collaboration.

11   For more practical literature on teamwork I am happy to refer you to:
Lencioni, P. (2005). *Overcoming the Five Dysfunctions of a Team. A Field Guide for Leaders, Managers and Facilitators*. San Francisco: Jossey-Bass.
Schwarz, R., Davidson, A., Carlson, P., & McKinney, S. (2005). *The Skilled Facilitator Fieldbook: Tips, Tools, and Tested Methods for Consultants, Facilitators, Trainers, and Coaches*. San Francisco: Jossey-Bass.

12   The Team Mirror is a project that was made possible thanks to the European Social Fund (ESF). http://ec.europa.eu/esf/home.jsp?langId=n

13   Decuyper, S., Dochy, F., & Van Den Bossche, P. (2010). Grasping the Dynamic Complexity of Team Learning: An Integrative Model for Effective Team Learning in Organisations. *Educational Research Review, 5* (2), 111-133. Elsevier Ltd. doi: 10.1016/j.edurev.2010.02.002.

[14] Senge, P. (1990). *The Fifth Discipline. The Art & Practice of the Learning Organization*. New York: Doubleday.

[15] Inspired by an analogy made by emeritus Prof. Dr. Herman Baert during a lecture at University of Leuven on 28/04/2018, referring to emeritus Prof. Dr. Jacques Stalpers.

[16] Quote downloaded on 26/08/2018 from https://www.brainyquote.com/quotes/albert_einstein_383803

[17] Inspired by an analogy made by Paul Stinckens, founder of Unicorn.

[18] Cohen, S.G. & Bailey, D.E. (1997). What Makes Teams Work: Group Effectiveness Research from the Shop Floor to the Executive Suite. *Journal of Management, 23* (3), 239-290.

[19] Edmondson, A.C. (2012). *Teaming: How Organizations Learn, Innovate, and Compete in the Knowledge Economy*. San Francisco: Jossey-Bass.

[20] Visited on 26/08/2018 via https://www.retentie-management.com/personeelsverloop-in-de-privesector/

[21] Salas, E., Rozell, D., Mullen, B. & Driskell, J.E. (1999). The Effect of Team Building on Performance: An Integration. *Small Group Research, 30* (3), 309-329. doi: 10.1177/104649649903000303.
Salas, E., Stagl, K.C. & Burke, C.S. (2004). 25 Years of Team Effectiveness in Organizations: Research Themes and Emerging Needs. *International Review of Industrial and Organizational Psychology*, 19, 47-92.
Klein, C., DiazGranados, D., Salas, E., Le, H., Burke, C.S., Lyons, R. & Goodwin, G.F. (2009). Does Team Building Work? *Small Group Research*, 40, 181- 222. doi: 10.1177/1046496408328821

[22] Remmerswaal, J. (1995). *Handboek Groepsdynamica. Een nieuwe inleiding op theorie en praktijk*. Soest: H. Nelissen.

[23] Thank you, Ignace Van Doorselaere and Janine Sloof for reminding us about the reality.

[24] Van Doorselaere, I. (2011). *En jij, waar vecht jij voor?* 4F Flexible Focus Fair Fight.

[25] Covey, S.R. (1989). *The Seven Habits of Highly Effective People*. New York: Simon & Schuster.

[26] Van Der Vurst, J. (2012). Impact. *Being right and being proven right. [Impact. Gelijk hebben en gelijk krijgen.]* Utrecht: Het Spectrum.

[27] Pausch, R. (2007). Randy Pausch's Last Lecture: Really Achieving Your Childhood Dreams. Visited on 29-08-2018 op https://www.cs.cmu.edu/~pausch/Randy/pauschlastlecturetranscript.pdf.

[28] Drucker, P.F. (2001). *A Century of Social Transformation - Emergence of a Knowledge Society. Hoofdstuk uit The Essential Drucker*. New York: HarperCollins Publishers.

[29] Sherman, J. R. (1982). *How to Survive Rejection*, Golden Valley: Pathway Books, p. 45.

[30] Koeslag-Kreunen , M., Van den Bossche, P., Hoven, M., Van der Klink, M. & Gijselaers, M. (2004). When Leadership Powers Team Learning: A Meta-Analysis. *Small Group Research* 49(4), 1–39. doi: i1.00r.g1/107.171/1770/41604694694614818776644824.

[31] Ancona, D., Bresman, H. & Kaeufer, K. (2002). The Comparative Advantage of X-Teams. *MIT Sloan Management Review, 43* (3), 33-39.

[32] Visited on 20/01/2019 via https://www.brainyquote.com/authors/socrates

[33] Thank you Unicorn for the cartoon and the metaphor. www.unicorngroup.be.

[34] Sanner, B. & Bunderson, J.S. (2015). When Feeling Safe Isn't Enough: Contextualizing Models of Safety and Learning in Teams. *Organizational Psychology Review*, 1-20. doi: 10.1177/2041386614565145.

[35] Covey, S.R. (1989). *The Seven Habits of Highly Effective People*. New York: Simon & Schuster. Nederlandse vertaling: *De zeven eigenschappen voor effectief leiderschap*. Amsterdam/ Antwerpen: Business Contact.

[36] Raes, E. (2015). *Team's Anatomy. Exploring Change in Teams*. Unpublished Doctoral Dissertation. University of Leuven.
Sessa, V.I. & London, M. (2008). Work Group Learning. *Understanding, Improving & Assessing How Groups Learn in Organizations*. Mahwah, New Jersey: Lawrence Erlbaum Associates.

[37] Koeslag-Kreunen, M., Van den Bossche, P., Hoven, M., Van der Klink, M. & Gijselaers, M. (2004). When Leadership Powers Team Learning: A Meta-Analysis. *Small Group Research*, 1-39. doi: 10.1177/1046496418764824.

[38] Revans, R.W. (1980). *Action Learning: New Techniques for Management*. London: Blond & Briggs.

[39] Hackman, J.R. & Wageman, R. (2005). A Theory of Team Coaching. *The Academy of Management Review, 30* (2), 269-287. doi: 10.2307/20159119.
Bunderson, J.S. & Sutcliffe, K.M. (2003). Management Team Learning Orientation and Business Unit Performance. *Journal of Applied Psychology, 88* (3), 552-560.
London, M. & Sessa, V.I. (2007). The Development of Group Interaction Patterns: How Groups Become Adaptive, Generative, and Transformative Learners. *Human Resource Development Review, 6* (4), 353-376. doi: 10.1177/1534484307307549.

[40] Decuyper, S., Dochy, F. & Van den Bossche, P. (2010). Grasping the Dynamic Complexity of Team Learning: An Integrative Model for Effective Team Learning in Organisations. *Educational Research Review, 5* (2): 111-133. doi:10.1016/j.edurev.2010.02.002.

[41] Jehn, K.A. & Rupert, J. (2008). Group Faultlines and Team Learning: How to Benefit from Different Perspectives. In Valerie Sessa & Manuel London (eds.): *Work Group Learning. Understanding, Improving & Assessing How Groups Learn in Organizations*. (p. 15-44). Mahwah, New Jersey: Lawrence Erlbaum Associates.

[42] London, M. & Sessa, V.I. (2007). How Groups Learn, Continuously. *Human Resource Management, 46* (4), 651-669. doi: 10.1002/hrm.

[43] Thank you, Wilfried Neven – CEO of Allianz Belgium – for giving me this insight.

[44] Thank you, Joris Roels from Unicorn, for introducing me to this concept.

[45] One of the pitfalls of communication is to stay stuck in your own frame of reference. It is possible that your colleague has a very different interpretation of the same words. Test it with this small experiment: ask a couple of people what it means when someone says 'I am running a bit late.' A frame of reference is a filter for translation and everybody has a different filter. So check your assumptions. Don't assume somebody understands you or vice versa.

[46] Kazl, E., Marsick, V.J. & Dechant, K. (1997). Teams as Learners. A Research-Based Model of Team Learning. *Journal of Applied Behavioural Science, 33* (2), 227-246.

[47] Van Den Bossche, P., Gijselaers, W.H., Segers, M. & Kirschner, P.A. (2006). Social and Cognitive Factors Driving Teamwork in Collaborative Learning Environments: Team Learning Beliefs and Behaviours. *Small Group Research, 37* (5), 490-521. doi: 10.1177/1046496406292938.

[48] Gill, J. (2016). *Fail Fast to Succeed,* TEDxTacoma. Visited on 29/08/2018 via https://www.youtube.com/watch?v=XJpnCLOooFE.

[49] Visited on 29/08/2018 via https://en.wikiquote.org/wiki/User:Grover_cleveland/Success_is_going_from_failure_to_failure_without_loss_of_enthusiasm.

[50] Wilson, J.M., Goodman, P.S. & Cronin, M.A. (2007). Group Learning. *Academy of Management Review, 32* (4), 1041-1059.

[51] London, M. & Sessa, V.I. (2006). Group Feedback for Continuous Learning. *Human Resource Development Review, 5*(3), 1-27.

[52] Gabelica, C. (2014). *Moving Teams Forward. Effects of Feedback and Team Reflexivity on Team Performance.* Unpublished dissertation. Maastricht University: Maastricht.

[53] ... and what about the facts? When giving feedback, it is always a good idea to focus on concrete facts. But be aware that these 'facts' are nothing more or less than 'your perception of the facts'.

[54] If you are interested in the real definition of feedback in teams: '*Feedback in teams has been conceptualized as the delivery of information on actions, events, or processes.*' From London, M. & Sessa, V.I. (2006). Group Feedback for continuous learning. *Human Resources Development Review, 5*(3), 1-27.

[55] Dochy, F., & Segers, M. (2018). *Creating Impact Through Future Learning: The High Impact Learning that Lasts (HILL) Model.* London: Routledge.

[56] Kerr, N.L., Messé, L.M., Park, E.S. & Sambolec, E. (2005). Identifiably, Performance Feedback and the Köhler Effect. *Group Processes and Intergroup Relations, 8* (4), 375-390.

[57] Thank you, Saïd Benali of BNP Paribas Fortis, who taught me this term during a Unicorn seminar.

[58] Kluger, A.N. & DeNisi, A. (1996). The Effects of Feedback Interventions on Performance: A Historical Review, a Meta-Analysis, and a Preliminary Feedback Intervention Theory. *Psychological Bulletin, 119,* 254-284.

[59] Also known as the feedback sandwich. A praxis that has no scientific value whatsoever. So, let's say goodbye to the sandwich.

[60] Gabelica, C., Van den Bossche, P., Segers, M. & Gijselaers, W. (2014). Dynamics of Team Reflexivity After Feedback. *Frontline Learning Research 5,* 64-91. issn 2295-3159.

[61] Edmondson, A.C. (1999). Psychological Safety and Learning Behaviour in Work Teams. *Administrative Science Quarterly, 44* (2), 350-383.

[62] Schein, E.H. (1993). How Can Organizations Learn Faster? The Challenge of Entering the Green Room. *Sloan Management Review, 34,* 85–92.
Kahn, W.A. (1990). Psychological Conditions of Personal Engagement and Disengagement at Work. *Academy of Management Journal, 33,* 692–724.

[63] Edmondson, A.C. (1996). Learning from Mistakes is Easier Said Than Done: Group and Organizational Influences on the Detection and Correction of Human Error. *The Journal of Applied Behavioural Science, 32* (1), 5-28. doi: 10.1177/0021886396321001.

64   Duhigg, C. (2016). What Google Learned From Its Quest to Build the Perfect Team. *The New York Times Magazine*, Feb. 25.

65   Sanner, B. & Bunderson, J.S. (2015). When Feeling Safe Isn't Enough: Contextualizing Models of Safety and Learning in Teams. *Organizational Psychology Review*, 1-20. doi: 10.1177/2041386614565145.

66   Frazier, M. L., Fainshmidt, S., Klinger, R. L., Pezeshkan, A., & Vracheva, V. (2017). Psychological safety: A meta-analytic review and extension. *Personnel Psychology*, 70(1), 113-165.

67   Edmondson, A.C. (2012). *Teaming. How Organizations Learn, Innovate, and Compete in the Knowledge Economy.* San Francisco: Wiley, Jossey-Bass.

68   Edmondson, A.C. (2008). The Competitive Imperative of Learning. *Harvard Business Review, 86*(7/8), 60-67. Retrieved on 23/07/2010 from http://www.rapsa.org/pdf/the_competitive_imperative_of_learning.pdf. p.65.

69   Edmondson, A.C. (2002). Managing the Risk of Learning: Psychological Safety in Work Teams. In West, M. (ed.). *International Handbook of Organizational Teamwork*, London: Blackwell.

70   Edmondson, A.C. & Lei, Z. (2014). Psychological Safety: The History, Renaissance, and Future of an Interpersonal Construct. *Annual Review of Organizational Psychology and Organizational Behavior, 1*, 23-43. doi: 10.1146/annurev-orgpsych-031413-091305.

71   Gurven, M. & Kaplan, H. (2007). Longevity Amongst Hunter-Gatherers. *Population and Development Review, 33* (2), 326. doi:10.1111/j.1728-4457.2007.00171.x.

72   Delizonna, L. (2017). High-Performing Teams Need Psychological Safety. Here's How to Create It. *Harvard Business Review, 24*, 1-5.

73   Ibid.

74   Edmondson, A.C. (2002). Managing the Risk of Learning. In West, M. (ed.). *International Handbook of Organizational Teamwork*. London: Blackwell.

75   Brown, B. (2013). *De kracht van kwetsbaarheid. Heb de moed om niet perfect te willen zijn.* Utrecht: A.W. Bruna.

76   Wheelan, S.A. & Mckeage, R.L. (1993). Developmental Patterns in Small and Large Groups. *Small Group Research, 24* (1), 60-76.

77   Van Den Bossche, P., Gijselaers, W.H., Segers, M. & Kirschner, P.A. (2006). Social and Cognitive Factors Driving Teamwork in Collaborative Learning Environments: Team Learning Beliefs and Behaviours. *Small Group Research, 37* (5), 490-521. doi: 10.1177/1046496406292938.

78   Edmondson, A.C. (2002). The Local and Variegated Nature of Learning in Organizations. *Organization Science, 13* (2), 128-146. doi: 10.1287/orsc.13.2.128.530.

79   Fredrickson, B.L. (2004). The Broaden-and-Build Theory of Positive Emotions. *Phil. Trans. R. Soc. Lond. B. 359*, 1367-1377. doi:10.1098/rstb.2004.1512.

80   Delizonna, L. (2017). High-Performing Teams Need Psychological Safety. Here's How to Create It. *Harvard Business Review, 24*, 1-5.

81   Miller, G.A. (1956). The Magical Number Seven, Plus or Minus Two: Some Limits on our Capacity for Processing Information. *Psychological Review, 63*, 81-97.http://psychclassics.yorku.ca/Miller/.

[82] Dee Hock, as cited in Allen, D. (2001). *Getting Things Done. The Art of Stress-Free Productivity*. London: Penguin.

[83] Thanks to Ignace Van Doorselaere – CEO of Neuhaus – for this insight. Website visited 12/02/2019 on https://www.tijd.be/opinie/algemeen/het-kader-mag-niet-belangrijker-worden-dan-het-schilderij/10004570.html.

[84] Edmondson, A.C. (2002b). Managing the Risk of Learning. In M. West (ed.). *International Handbook of Organizational Teamwork*. London: Blackwell.

[85] Quote attributed to Jerry Belson. Downloaded 20-01-2019 on https://en.wikipedia.org/wiki/Jerry_Belson.

[86] Raes, E., Boon, A., Kyndt, E. & Dochy, F. (2015). Measuring Team Learning Behaviours Through Observing Verbal Team Interaction. *Journal of Workplace Learning, 27*, 476-500. doi:10.1108/JWL-01-2015-0006.

[87] Covey, S.R. (1989). *The Seven Habits of Highly Effective People*. New York: Simon & Schuster.

[88] Edmondson, A.C. (2011). Strategies for Learning from Failure. *Harvard Business Review*. Visited March 31st 2020 on https://hbr.org/2011/04/strategies-for-learning-from-failure.

[89] Edmondson, A.C. (2012). *Teaming. How Organizations Learn, Innovate, and Compete in the Knowledge Economy*. San Francisco: Wiley, Jossey-Bass.

[90] At the basis of this misconception is a mindset that Carol Dweck refers to as a *fixed mindset*. Would you like to learn more about fixed mindsets and how they differ from a growth mindset? We focus on this topic in Chapter 6: Individual Impact.

[91] Brown, B. (2012). *The Power of Vulnerability: Teachings on Authenticity, Connection, & Courage*. Available at: https://www.soundstrue.com/store/the-power-of-vulnerability-2917.html.

[92] Ibid.

[93] Ibid.

[94] https://en.wikipedia.org/wiki/Pierre_de_Coubertin.

[95] Story by Paul Stinckens, founder of Unicorn.

[96] DeChurch, L.A. & Mesmer-Magnus, J.R. (2010). The Cognitive Underpinnings of Effective Teamwork: A Meta-Analysis. *Journal of Applied Psychology, 95* (1), 32-53.

[97] Visited 12/02/2019 on https://www.dictionary-quotes.com/if-everyone-is-thinking-alike-then-somebody-isn-t-thinking-george-s-patton.

[98] I would recommend this thinking exercise to everybody who writes or presents. Thank you, Pauline Appels, for your curious question.

[99] Mohammed, S., Ferzandi L. & Hamilton, K. (2010). Metaphor No More: A 15-Year Review of the Team Mental Model Construct. *Journal of Management, 36* (4), 876-910. doi:10.1177/0149206309356804.

[100] Kleingeld, A., van Mierlo, H. & Arends., L. (2011). The Effect of Goal Setting on Group Performance: A Meta-Analysis. *Journal of Applied Psychology, 96* (6), 1289-1204. doi: 10.1037/a0024315.

[101] Senge, P. (1990). *The Fifth Discipline. The Art & Practice of the Learning Organization*. New York: Doubleday.

[102] Senge, P.M. (1990). The Leadership's New Work: Building Learning Organisations. *Sloan Management Review*, 32 (1), 7-23.

[103] Banks, A.P. & McKeran, W.J. (2005). Team Situation Awareness, Shared Displays and Performance. *International Journal of Cognitive Technology*, 10: 23-28.

[104] Salas, E., Sims, D.E. & Burke, C.S. (2005). Is There a 'Big Five' in Teamwork? *Small Group Research*, 36 (5), 555-599. doi: 10.1177/1046496405277134.

[105] Lammers, M. (2015). *Yes! Een Crisis. Top Coaches*. Baarn: Tirion Sport.

[106] Ellis, A.P.J., Porter, C. O.L.H. & Wolverton, S.A. (2008). Learning to Work Together: An Examination of Transactive Memory System Development in Teams. In Valerie Sessa & Manuel London (eds.). *Work Group Learning. Understanding, Improving & Assessing How Groups Learn in Organizations* (p. 15-44). Mahwah, New Jersey: Lawrence Erlbaum Associates.

[107] Huckman, R.S., Bradley, R.S. & Staats, D.M.U. (2009). Team familiarity, role experience, and performance: evidence from indivian software services. *Management Science*, 55(1), 85-100.

[108] Covey, S.R. (1989). *The Seven Habits of Highly Effective People*. New York: Simon & Schuster. Summary of Recent Goals Research by Gail Matthews, PhD., Dominican University. Visited 19/01/2019 on https://sidsavara.com/wp-content/uploads/2008/09/researchsummary2.pdf.

[109] Loehr, J. (2007). *The Power of Story. Change Your Story, Change Your Destiny in Business and in Life*. New York: Free Press.

[110] Ibid.

[111] Lammers, M. (2015). *Yes! Een Crisis. Top Coaches [Yes! A crisis! Top Coaches]*. Baarn: Tirion Sport.

[112] West, M. (2004). Do Teams Work? In M. West, *Effective Teamwork. Practical Lessons From Organizational Research* (pp. 7-26). Leicester: Blackwell.
This model was designed and developed by Unicorn. At Unicorn, they call it the Winning Team model, because High Impact Teams are labeled Winning Teams.

[113] Cumps, J. (2018). *Sociocratie 3.0. De business novelle die het beste uit mens en organisatie haalt [Sociocracy 3.0. The business short story that brings out the best in people and organizations]*. Tielt: Lannoo Campus.

[114] West, M. (2004). Do Teams Work? In M. West, *Effective Teamwork. Practical Lessons from Organizational Research* (p. 7-26). Leicester: Blackwell.

[115] Gilovich, T., Savitsky, K., & Medvec, V.(1998). The Illusion of Transparency: Biased Assessments of Others' Ability to Read One's Emotional States. *Journal of Personality and Social Psychology*, 75 (2), 332-346. doi:10.1037/0022-3514.75.2.332.

[116] This feedback exercise was originally developed by Unicorn, and is called the 'Gossip exercise'.

[117] Kimsey-House, H., Kimsey-House, K., Sandahl, P. & Whitworth, L. (2011). *Co-active Coaching: Changing Business Transforming Lives*. Boston: Nicholas Brealey Publishing.

[118] Ibid.

[119] Visited on 12/02/2019 via http://meaningring.com/2015/04/17/daily-rituals-kant-by-mason-currey.

[120] Hackman, J.R., Wageman, R., Ruddy, T.M. & Ray, C.R. (2000). Team Effectiveness in Theory and Practice. In C. Cooper & E.A. Locke (eds.). *Industrial and Organizational Psychology: Theory and Practice*: 109-129. Oxford: Blackwell.

[121] Wageman, R. (2001). How Leaders Foster Self-Managing Team Effectiveness: Design Choices vs. Hands-On Coaching. *Organization Science, 12* (5), 559-577. doi: 10.1287/orsc.12.5.559.10094.

[122] Allen, D. (2001). *Getting Things Done. The Art of Stress-Free Productivity*. New York: Penguin. Nederlandse vertaling: *Getting Things Done*. Utrecht: A.W. Bruna.

[123] Maenen, S. (2018). *Van Babel tot Ontwerp. Concepten en methoden voor het ontwikkelen van organisaties*. Kalmthout: Pelckmans Pro.

[124] Covey, S.R. (1989). *The Seven Habits of Highly Effective People*. New York: Simon & Schuster. Nederlandse vertaling: *De zeven eigenschappen voor effectief leiderschap*. Amsterdam/ Antwerpen: Business Contact.

[125] Blake, N., Smeyers, P., Smith, R. & Standish, P. (1998). *Thinking Again. Education after Postmodernism*. Westport: Bergin & Garvey.

[126] van Mierlo, H., Rutte. C.G. Vermunt, J.K., Kompier, M.A.J. & Doorewaard, J.A.M.C. (2006). Individual Autonomy in Work Teams: The Role of Team Autonomy, Self-Efficacy, and Social Support. *European Journal of Work and Organizational Psychology, 15* (3), 281-299. doi: 10.1080/13594320500412249.

[127] Morgeson, F.P., DeRue, D.S. & Karam, E.P. (2010). Leadership in Teams: A Functional Approach to Understanding Leadership Structures and Processes. *Journal of Management, 36* (1), 5-39. doi: 10/1177/0149206309347376.

[128] Seligman, M.E.P. (1975). *Helplessness: On Depression, Development, and Death*. San Francisco: W. H. Freeman.

[129] Mischel, W. (2014). *The Marshmallow Test: Mastering Self-Control*. New York: Little, Brown Spark.

[130] Kotter, J. P. (1996). *Leading Change*. Boston: Harvard Business School Press.

[131] Duhigg, C. 2008. Warning: Habits may be good for you. *New York Times* (July 13), http://www.nytimes.com/2008/07/13/business/13habit.html.

[132] Allen, D. (2001). *Getting Things Done. The Art of Stress-Free Productivity*. New York: The Penguin Group.

[133] Koeslag-Kreunen, M., Van den Bossche, P., Hoven, M., Van der Klink, M. & Gijselaers, M. (2004). When Leadership Powers Team Learning: A Meta-Analysis. *Small Group Research. 49* (4), 475-513. doi:10.1177/1046496418764824.

[134] Pearce, C. L. & Sims, H.P. (2002). Vertical Versus Shared Leadership as Predictors of the Effectiveness of Change Management Teams: An Examination of Aversive, Directive, Transactional, Transformational, and Empowering Leader Behaviors. *Group Dynamics: Theory, Research, and Practice, 6* (2), 172-197. doi:10.1037//1089-2699.6.2.172.

[135] In the research of Pearce & Sims (2002), shared leadership is even a stronger determinant for High Impact Teaming: it explains more variance in team effectiveness than 'heroic' (vertical) leadership.

136 Hoch, J.E., Bommer, W.H., Dulebohn, J.H. & Wu, D. (2018). Do Ethical, Authentic, and Servant Leadership Explain Variance Above and Beyond Transformational Leadership? A Meta-Analysis, *Journal of Management*, 44(2), 501-529. doi:10.1177/0149206316665461.

137 Van Loon, R. (2006). *Het geheim van de leider*. *[The leader's secret]* Assen: Van Gorcum.

138 Cialdini, R.B. (2007). *Influence. The Psychology of Persuasion*. New York: Collins Business. Nederlandse vertaling: *Invloed*. Amsterdam: Boom.

139 Van Houtem, G. (2010). *De Dirty Tricks van het onderhandelen. Ontdek de regels van het spel en verbeter je machtspositie [The Dirty Tricks of negotiation. Get to know the rules, and improve your position of power.]*. Zaltbommel: Haystack.

140 Van Der Vurst, J. (2012). *Impact. Gelijk hebben en gelijk krijgen [Impact. Be right and be proved right]*. Utrecht: Het Spectrum.

141 Covey, S.R. (1989). *The Seven Habits of Highly Effective People*. New York: Simon & Schuster. Nederlandse vertaling: *De zeven eigenschappen voor effectief leiderschap*. Amsterdam/Antwerpen: Business Contact.

142 Derks, L. & Hollander, J. (2012). *Essenties van nlp. Sleutels tot persoonlijke verandering [The essence of NLP. Keys to personal change]*. Utrecht: Kosmos.

143 Frankl, V.E. (2006). *Man's Search For Meaning*. Boston: Beacon Press (p. 66).

144 Dweck, C.S. (2006). *Mindset. The New Psychology of Success. How We Can Learn to Fulfill Our Potential*. New York: Ballantine Books.

145 Blackwell, L.S., Trzesniewski, K.H. & Dweck, C.S. (2007). Implicit Theories of Intelligence Predict Achievement Across an Adolescent Transition: A Longitudinal Study and an Intervention. *Child Development*, 78 (1), 246-263.
Cury, F., Da Fonseca, D., Zahn, Z. & Elliot, A. (2008). Implicit Theories and IQ Test Performance: A Sequential Mediational Analysis. *Journal of Experimental Social Psychology*, 44 , 783-791.
Haimovitz, K., Wormington, S.V. & Corpus, J.H. (2011). Dangerous Mindsets: How Beliefs About Intelligence Predict Motivational Change. *Learning and Individual Differences*, 21 (2011), 747–752.

146 Dweck, C.S. (2006). *Mindset. The New Psychology of Success. How We Can Learn to Fulfill Our Potential*. New York: Ballantine Books.

147 Ibid.

148 Heslin, P.A. & Keating, L.A. (2017). In a Learning Mode? The Role of Mindsets in Derailing and Enabling Experiential Leadership Development. *The Leadership Quarterly*, 28 (3), 367-384. doi:10.1016/j.leaqua.2016.10.010.

149 Lencioni, P. (2005). *Overcoming the Five Dysfunctions of a Team. A Field Guide for Leaders, Managers and Facilitators*. San Francisco: Jossey-Bass.

150 Covey, S.R. (1989). *The Seven Habits of Highly Effective People*. New York: Simon & Schuster.

151 Kimsey-House, H., Kimsey-House, K., Sandahl, P. & Witworth, L. (2011). *Co-active Coaching: Changing Business Transforming Lives*. Boston: Nicholas Brealey Publishing.

152 Senge, P.M. (1990). *The Fifth Discipline. The Art & Practice of the Learning Organization*. New York: Currency Doubleday.

153 https://www.ted.com/talks/worklife_with_adam_grant_how_astronauts_build_trust?referrer=playlist-worklife_with_adam_grants.

[154] Senge, P.M. (1990). *The Fifth Discipline. The Art & Practice of the Learning Organization*. New York: Doubleday.

[155] Senge, P.M. (1990). The Leadership's New Work: Building Learning Organisations. *Sloan Management Review, 32* (1), 7-23.

[156] STEP at the individual level was developed by Joris Roels, Paul Stinckens, Claudia Straetemans and Emilie Schollaert, partners of Unicorn. (www.unicorngroup.be). It is sometimes referred to as *Value Based Leadership*.

[157] Millman, D. (1980). *Way of the Peaceful Warrior: A Book That Changes Lives*. Novato: New World Library.

[158] Sentence based on the following quote 'Energy, not time, is the fundamental currency of high performance.' Uit: Loehr, J. & Schwartz, T. (2001). The Making of a Corporate Athlete. *Harvard Business Review*.

[159] Loehr, J. & Schwartz, T. (2001). The Making of a Corporate Athlete. *Harvard Business Review*.

[160] Covey, S.R. (1989). *The Seven Habits of Highly Effective People*. New York: Simon & Schuster.

[161] Niebuhr, R. (1951). The Serenity Prayer.

[162] Dobelli, R. (2011). *The art of thinking clearly*. New York: HarperCollins Publisher.

[163] Dechant, K., Marsick, V. J., & Kasl, E. (1993). Towards a model of team learning. *Studies in Continuing Education, 15*(1), 1–14.

[164] Rubin, I., Plovnick, M., & Fry, R. (1974) Initiating planned change in health care systems. *Journal of Applied Behavioral Science (10)*,107-124.

[165] VUCA, an acronym that originated in the US military in the late '90s, stands for Volatile, Uncertain, Complex and Ambiguous, and found its way into business lexicon a decade ago. A VUCA context is said to make confident diagnosis and certain decisions near impossible. For more information about the impact of VUCA on different aspects of performance, see Bennett, N. & Lemoine, G.J. (2014). What a difference a word makes: Understanding threats to performance in a VUCA world, *Business Horizons*, 57(3), 311-317. doi:10.1016/j. bushor.2014.01.00

[166] Argyris, C. & Schön, D. A. (1996). *Organizational learning II: Theory method and practice*. Reading, MA: Addison-Wesley.

[167] Nielsen, R. P. (1993b). Woolman's "I am we" triple-loop action-learning: Origin and application in organization ethics. *Journal of Applied Behavioral Science, 29*(1), 117-138.

[168] Eynikel, J. (2019). Check-In. Op zoek naar zin en betekenis in bedrijven. Leuven: LannooCampus.

[169] Deutsch, M. (1962). *Cooperation and Trust: Some Theoretical Notes*. In M.R. Jones (ed.), Nebraska Symposium on Motivation, 275-319. Lincoln: University of Nebraska Press.

[170] Balliet, D. & Van Lange, P.A.M. (2013). Trust, Conflict, and Cooperation: A Meta-Analysis. *Psychological Bulletin, 139* (5), 1090–1112. doi: 10.1037/a0030939.
O'Boyle, E.H., Humphrey, R.H., Pollack, J.M., Hawver, T.H. & Story, P.A. (2005). The Relation Between Emotional Intelligence and Job Performance: A Meta-Analysis. *Journal of Organizational Behavior, 32*, 788–818 (2011). doi: 10.1002/job.714.

[171] Zak, P., Kurzband, R. & Matznere, W. (2005). Oxytocin Is Associated With Human Trustworthiness. In: *Hormones and Behavior, 48* (2005), 522-527.

[172] Van IJzendoorn, M.H., & Bakermans-Kranenburg, M.J. (2012). A Sniff of Trust: Meta-Analysis of the Effects of Intranasal Oxytocin Administration on Face Recognition, Trust to In-Group, and Trust to Out-Group. In: *Psychoneuroendocrinology 37,* (2012), 438-443. doi:10.1016/j. psyneuen.2011.07.008.

[173] Covey, S.M.R. (2008). *The Speed of Trust.* New York: Simon & Schuster.

[174] Kosfeld, M., Heinrichs, M., Zak, P.J., Fischbacher, U. & Fehr, E. (2005). Oxytocin Increases Trust in Humans. *Nature, 453,* 637-676.

[175] Zak, P.J., Kurzban, R. & Matzner, W.T. (2005). Oxytocin Is Associated With Human Trustworthiness. *Hormones & Behavior, 48,* 522-527. doi: 10.1016/j.yhbeh.2005.07.2009.

[176] De Dreu, C.K.W., Greer, Van Kleef, G.A., Shalvi, S., & Handgraaf M.J.J. (2011). *Oxytocin promotes human ethnocentrism. Proceedings of the National Academy of Sciences of the United States of America, 108 (4),* 1262-1266.

[177] Covey, S.M.R. (2008). *The Speed of Trust.* New York: Simon & Schuster.

[178] Sundstrom, E., McIntyre, M., Halfhill, T. & Richards, H. (2000). Work Groups: From the Hawthorne Studies to Work Teams of the 1990s and Beyond. *Group Dynamics: Theory, Research, and Practice, 4 (1),* 44-67. doi: 10.1037//1089-2699.4.
Gully, S.M., Incalcaterra, K.A., Joshi, A. & Beaubien, J.M. (2002). A Meta-Analysis of Team Efficacy, Potency, and Performance: Interdependence and Level of Analysis as Moderators of Observed Relationships. *Journal of Applied Psychology, 87* (5), 819-832.

[179] Mullen, B. & Copper, C. (1994). The Relation Between Group Cohesiveness and Performance: An Integration. *Psychological Bulletin, 115* (2), 210-227.

[180] Johnson, D.W. & Johnson, R.T. (2003). Training For Cooperative Group Work. In M.A. West, D. Tjosvold & K.G. Smith (eds.). *International Handbook of Organizational Teamwork And Cooperative Working.* London: Blackwell.

[181] Thank you, Wilfried Neven – CEO of Allianz Belgium – for this insight.

[182] Covey, S.M.R. (2008). *The Speed of Trust.* New York: Simon & Schuster.

[183] Oxfam Briefing Paper (January 2018). *Reward Work, Not Wealth.* Bezocht op 9/08/2018 van: https://d1tn3vj7xz9fdh.cloudfront.net/s3fs-public/file_attachments/bp-reward-work-not-wealth-220118-en.pdf.

[184] United Nations Statistics Division (2015). *The World's Women Trends and Statistics.* Visited 9/08/18 at: https://unstats.un.org/unsd/gender/worldswomen.html.

[185] United Nations Environment (2018). *The State of Plastics.* Visited 19/08/2018 at: https://wedocs.unep.org/bitstream/handle/20.500.11822/25513/state_plastics_WED. pdf?isAllowed=y&sequence=1.

[186] United Nations Environment (2017). *The Emission Gap Report.* Visited 19/08/2018 at: https://wedocs.unep.org/bitstream/handle/20.500.11822/22070/EGR_2017. pdf?isAllowed=y&sequence=1.

[187] Bezocht op 20/01/2019 op: https://www.brainyquote.com/authors/margaret_mead.

[188] Harvey, J.B. (1974). The Abilene Paradox: The Management of Agreement. *Organizational Dynamics, 3* (1), 63-80.

[189] De Coster, M. (2012). *No Nonsense. Brains. Heart. Guts. Troeven van de manager. [No Nonsense. Brains. Heart. Guts. Trumps of a manager.]* Tielt: LannooCampus.

[190] Bezocht op 20/01/2019 op: https://www.brainyquote.com/authors/margaret_mead.